FAERIES
NATURE SPIRITS
 a beginner's guide

TERESA MOOREY

Hodder & Stoughton
A MEMBER OF THE HODDER HEADLINE GROUP

Orders: please contact Bookpoint Ltd, 39 Milton Park, Abingdon, Oxon OX14 4TD. Telephone: (44) 01235 400414, Fax: (44) 01235 400454. Lines are open from 9.00–6.00, Monday to Saturday, with a 24-hour message answering service. Email address: orders@bookpoint.co.uk

British Library Cataloguing in Publication Data
A catalogue record for this title is available from The British Library

ISBN 0 340 75359 5

First published 1999
Impression number 10 9 8 7 6 5 4 3 2 1
Year   2005 2004 2003 2002 2001 2000 1999

Typeset by Transet Limited, Coventry, England.
Printed in Great Britain for Hodder & Stoughton Educational, a division of Hodder Headline plc, 338 Euston Road, London NW1 3BH by Cox and Wyman Limited, Reading, Berks.

For Lily Amber, may your life be filled with magic.
And for her mum, Lucy, with thanks.

Many thanks to Graham Boston for permission to quote his experience.

Thanks to all writers quoted in this work, for permission to use their material, with very special thanks to Claire Nahmad, for her contribution.

All efforts have been made to trace copyright holders. The author and publisher apologise for any inadvertent omission and if informed of such will be pleased to rectify this in subsequent editions.

CONTENTS

INTRODUCTION

The host is rushing 'twixt night and day
And where is there hope or deed as fair?
Caoilte tossing his burning hair
And Niamh calling Away, come away

Yeats, *The Hosting of the Sidhe*

The entrances to the World of Faerie are elusive and, if we once find one, we may return on a cold morning to find it gone, leaving us in the greyness of our mortality. And yet there are many Faerie portals; in the twisted claw of a tree-root, shimmering where a sunbeam earths itself amid beech trees, around the other side of the barrow-mound – always around the other side. We catch echoes of faery music or glimpse the grace of their movements from the corner of the eye, for only to rare mortals and at rare times do the Fair Folk manifest in their brilliance. Our 'reality' is too stodgy a medium for their delicacy.

Tales about faeries, and discussions of what they may truly be, are many and varied. Stories also recount how they are departing from the Earth, for since the time of Chaucer their numbers have been declining. In *A Book of Fairies* Katherine Briggs tells how faeries left the Lowlands of Scotland in the nineteenth century, for the last time. In a Scottish hamlet, one Sunday, when most of the villagers were at church, a boy and his sister spotted a diminutive cavalcade winding its way down from the hills and heading southward. They watched in astonishment as tiny riders on miniature ponies paraded soundlessly past them. At length the boy cried out to the last rider, 'Who are ye, and where go ye?' 'I am not of the race of Adam,' came the reply, 'and the People of Peace shall never more be seen in Scotland.'

1

However, the Celts do not readily relinquish their faeries and there are countless tales worldwide of faery encounters. To the Irish, faeries are a part of life and always have been. Our adoption of a rationalistic outlook has put blinkers on us, but fashions change and people are now seeing and sensing faeries in growing numbers, as consciousness alters. Some believe these beings are the spirits of Nature, with whom we need to work, to heal our world. Others say they are aliens, coming with important messages from other civilizations. Still others regard them as angels, demons or figments of the imagination. However, whether we speak of inner or outer reality, faeries are not to be ignored. Their characteristics seem to have changed little down the ages.

Faeries may be helpful and benevolent, puckish and unpredictable, wise, enchanting, terrifying and remote. Can we bring ourselves closer to the Faerie realm? And is this a desirable thing to attempt? What have been the experiences of the traditional travellers to Faerie? What can we learn about our world, by contact with Otherworld?

In the following pages we shall be looking at faeries in their many moods and manifestations, exploring what they may be and where they can be found. One thing is certain: faeries have not disappeared from the world, only from our eyes. If we seek to expand our perceptions we must go back to that oldest and simplest of sources, Nature itself, for our sight is given depth and clarity by contact with soil, leaf, root, stream and breeze.

Contact with the faeries starts within the soul.

Please note: The spelling 'faery' is preferred in this book, because it denotes real beings as opposed to the fairies of children's fiction. 'Faerie' is a term for the Otherworld, the Land of the Faeries.

The spelling 'fairy' is retained where it it quoted in sayings, poems, case studies (e.g. the Cottingley Fairies) and titles of films, books. etc., and in place names.

ENCOUNTERS WITH
THE FAERY FOLK

Up the airy mountain
Down the rushy glen
We daren't go a-hunting
For fear of little men

William Allingham, *The Fairies*

'Do you believe in fairies?' There are many people who would answer a definite 'yes' because they have actually seen them. If we are honest, most of us who have spent time alone and aware, in nature, have felt their presence and glimpsed them. However, we are taught these days to believe in only one reality, the down-to-earth material reality, that we believe is unchanging and reliable – until it is touched by faery fingers. If we are to make sense of our knowledge of faeries we need to examine the available possibilities, not with an eye to 'proving' they exist, for I do not believe we can ever do that to the confirmed sceptic, but with a view to being clear about what we mean and alive to the many different types of possible faery and beings that may appear faery-like but are something different.

Here is a review of possible definitions of faeries.

1   They are merely a product of the imagination in the most frivolous sense, being at best a diversion and at worst a dangerous delusion for minds that can't or won't cope with reality. In this category we might include accounts of faeries that are quite consciously 'made-up' in order to get attention and faeries spotted on the stagger back from the local bar!

4

2 They are 'imaginary' in a more positive sense and, as such, useful to Jungian psychologists who see them as powerful symbols arising from the Collective Unconscious. Thus, when these symbols enter our lives in some form, they have important meanings for us that we can and should examine creatively.

3 They are, in fact, the souls of the dead, ghosts and shades of the departed. This idea, in itself, has several ramifications. Many tales recount people taken bodily into Faerieland, who thus became as ghosts, riding with the faeries and passing into the hollow hills with the faery host. The studies of Evans Wentz (see Further Reading) indicated that, in Celtic areas, the domain of the dead was very often equated with Faerie. The other, simpler view is that accounts of faeries are just encounters with those who have departed this life but have not 'moved on' to other realms, remaining instead Earthbound. This takes us into the complex question of what exactly is a ghost...

4 They are angels, often at the lower end of the angelic hierarchy, here to watch over us, to bless and guard us.

5 They are devils in disguise, primed to tempt and corrupt, to entrap the soul so it may never enter paradise, and to cause all manner of mischief.

6 They are neither angel nor devil, but something in between (although rather closer to the devilish than the angelic) that got 'caught' on this Earth plane and are best avoided.

7 They are beings inhabiting parallel dimensions (although often, for some reason, having a great interest in our own world) that appear from time to time, when an interdimensional 'warp' occurs.

8 They are beings from other planets, that land in UFOs.

9 They are nature spirits, subtle beings within the world of Nature that look after plants, trees and the natural world in general.

10 They are elementals, which is similar to the above, but not quite the same, for the elementals are more the outbreath of natural energies, a living embodiment on the subtle planes of the states of matter.

11 They are pagan gods, goddesses, heroes and heroines. If you are a pagan you will probably see these beings as possessing a reality. If not, the old ways may be seen as surviving in faery lore.

12 They are/were real, solid creatures, similar to pygmies. Folklore accounts arise from times when these beings still survived. Possibly a handful do still live in remote areas (here we are in the same territory as Bigfoot and the Yeti). This is a possibility, but to date archaeological evidence does not support the idea of an earlier, diminutive race inhabiting Britain and Ireland. However, the pygmy tribes who still live in some parts of the world do have their own 'faery traditions'.

13 They are animals, or birds, seen in a half-light by someone who is fearful, fanciful or drugged.

Although this is quite a long list, there may be other possibilities. In addition, many faery tales are, no doubt, a spinning together of several categories. Let us now look at a selection of real encounters with faeries.

Lady Fanshaw and the Banshee

The banshee is an eerie figure from Irish lore. Her hair is long, her cloak is green and her eyes are a livid red, from endless weeping. More properly spelt *bean sidhe* she is of the people of the Sidhe (pronounced 'shee'). The Sidhe are Irish faeries, who some say are the pre-Celtic peoples who slid mysteriously into another dimension, leaving behind their magical heritage. These are also called the Tuatha de Danaan, the people of the Goddess Dana – a powerful and enchanted race who inhabited Eire before the Milesians landed and who subsequently struggled with, seduced and inspired their Celtic heirs. On winter nights, when the wind keened around the hilltop where we lived, I would block my ears against the wail of the banshee that my Irish father told me could be heard crying when a family member was about to die. On hearing of the death of my uncle, my father said sadly, 'It was the banshee I heard that night.' The banshee is still heard by certain Irish families, including some who have emigrated to the United States and elsewhere, for the land of Faerie is a little bit closer to those with Celtic heritage, wherever they may be.

Having said this, there are also indications that seers and their faery helpers are linked to the land. Uprooted seers may lose 'the sight' and contact with their faery co-walkers, at least for a while. There is a moving account of this, extracted from an eighteenth-century journal, given by R.J. Stewart in *The Living World of Faery* listed in Further Reading. '...these cousins (i.e. faery co-walkers of the Native Americans) would not speak with me for I was a stranger in their land... just as I could not see them, they could not see me, for my substance was of Uist, my home island... None of my own darlings crossed the dark waters with me... and I was alone.' Such were the words of a Scottish seer, taken to Virginia in a prison ship, who later succeeded in partly regaining his powers.

The experience of Lady Fanshaw is recounted by Katherine Briggs (see Further Reading). She lived between 1625 and 1676 and her encounter was a vivid one, occurring when she was visiting with Lady Honor O'Brian. She was woken in the small hours by a strange sound. Drawing back the curtains she saw, in the moonlight, a woman with red hair and a face of ghastly pallor leaning in through the window. After saying 'A horse' three times the woman vanished, as if her body were vapour. Lady Fanshaw's hair stood on end and she woke her husband. There was no more sleep that night for Lady Fanshaw or her husband and, as morning dawned, Lady O'Brian came in to them to say that she had been up all night tending a dying kinsman who had passed away at two in the morning. She expressed the hope that there had been no disturbance because the custom was that, when a family member was on her or his death-bed, the shape of a woman appeared each night at the window, until the person was dead. Many years in the past this woman had been seduced by a member of the O'Brian family, who, on finding her pregnant, murdered her and threw her into the river beneath the window. Not surprisingly, Lady Fanshaw and her husband made a hasty departure, being of the opinion that Irish superstition made them a prey to the wiles of the devil!

What are we to make of this? Was this a simple haunting, glamourized by tales of the banshee? Or do the people of the Sidhe give such mournful tasks to Earthbound spirits of the dead? Perhaps this was the banshee herself, mistaken for the dead girl. Some accounts of

banshees describe them as being the manifestation of a young girl of the family who died and, often, the banshee is a woman who died in childbirth. The word 'horse' is interesting, for the horse has long been considered capable of riding between the worlds. Perhaps Lady Fanshaw was mistaken and the word was 'hearse'. Or was this just a bad dream of Lady Fanshaw's, based on stories of the O'Brian family that she had heard before, but forgotten? Sceptics would say the latter.

Jeladevata

A more up-to-date encounter occurred in 1992 in West Bengal. A boy of five called Bhagavat was lost while swimming in a river with companions. Frantic to find him, his family searched everywhere until one of them spotted him, where the current was moving swiftly, just his finger sticking up out of the water. They dragged him out and found him quite unharmed, although he had been under the water for ten minutes.

His mother, relieved and amazed, asked him what had happened and he replied, 'I was swept under by the current but a beautiful lady held me up until I was rescued. She was dressed like a princess, wearing a crown and earrings.'

In that area there is an ancient tradition of an elfin creature who dwells in rivers and lakes and protects those in danger of drowning, called a Jeladevata. A similar incident happened in Peru in 1977 when Jorge Alvarez fell into a swamp and gave himself up for lost. But as he sank, four little beings appeared, looking like humans of about a metre (3 feet) in height, but with only three fingers and covered in green scales. These held out branches to him and pulled him to safety but, by the time he had recovered, they had vanished. These stories, given in *Alien Impact* by Michael Craft (St. Martin's, 1996) are in contrast to certain tales that tell of the dangerous seductiveness of water-spirits who, in the tradition of the sirens, lure the unwary to a watery grave through tricks and wiles or the transcendent beauty of their singing.

UFO ENTITIES

A detailed report comes from the experience of Mrs Hingley on
4 January, 1979, in Rowley Regis, England and is reported by Janet
Bord (see Further Reading). After seeing her husband off to work at
6:00 a.m. Mrs Hingley went to investigate a strange orange light and
saw a large sphere suspended over the garden. 'Three small figures
shot past her into the house: they were about 1 metre (3.5 feet) tall,
wore silvery tunics and transparent helmets "like goldfish bowls"
and also had large oval "wings" seemingly made of thin paper and
decorated with glittering dots.' These creatures had halos and their
limbs were silvery green, ending in tapering points with no hands or
feet. They told Mrs Hingley that they came from the sky, everything
they said was in unison, and they pressed buttons on their tunics as
if they were a translation device. They kept shining a light at her but
assured her that they meant her no harm. Things they touched lifted
up. When they asked for water Mrs Hingley gave it to them and,
although the glasses were returned empty, they were not seen to
drink. Taking one of the mince-pies also offered to them, they
returned to their craft and shot off. For the rest of the day Mrs
Hingley felt very ill and she suffered from headaches for some time
after the incident. Electrical items in the house that the creatures
had touched were damaged, some irreparably, as if they had been in
contact with a strong magnetic field and marks were left on the grass
where the 'craft' had been stationed.

Although the above account sounds bizarre, there is no reason to
regard it as a fabrication. Indeed it could not be entirely, because of
the evidence left by the encounter. There are any number of similar
accounts of encounters with 'extra-terrestrials' to the point where the
modern 'close encounter' has become the, marginally, acceptable
side of faery lore. The above description of the beings, small,
diaphanous and flying has much in common with the traditional
faery and there is much in the vast body of ufology that resembles
faery descriptions. Small stature, green colour and the ability to fly,
or at least 'glide', are common descriptions of the entities. 'Little
green men' may be a cliché, but they do figure in numerous accounts.
Another feature not, apparently, applicable in the above tale but

very common in both faery and UFO encounters is that of time-distortion, where the contactee or abductee finds they have 'lost' hours, or even days. This was immortalized in Washington Irving's story of Rip van Winkle, where a lazy farmer joins the dwarves at play, drinks their liquor and falls asleep. When he wakes up, his beard is long and grey and he is old. He returns to his village to find a generation has passed and he has been forgotten. This story was based on local legends of little men, although these can hardly be said to be confined to the Hudson Valley.

Therefore, the old accounts of faeries could be stories of extra-terrestrials, misinterpreted by the primitive peasantry of yesteryear. Or current accounts of extra-terrestrials could be merely a description of faeries that is more acceptable to modern thought. Possibly both are true. Who are we to limit and circumscribe the possibilities of faery entities?

(DORE ENCOUNTERS

The connection of faeries with dancing is well known, for they are often to be seen dancing in 'faery-rings' and humans were reputed to be lured to their destruction by faeries who danced them to death in their circle. One account given by Evans Wentz (see Further Reading) has a rather different twist, in that the woman in question died while dancing on her wedding night. Soon after her death she appeared to her husband telling him she was not really dead but taken away from him for a period of time. She told him that she could see him but he did not see her and that if he wished to get her back he must stand at the gap near the house and catch her as she went by. Because he loved her he went straight to the gap, where a company of strangers were just coming out. His wife appeared soon, quite plainly, but he found himself unable to stir, hand or foot. She gave a scream and was gone, lost to him forever. He never married again.

Two, more cheerful, accounts are given by Janet Bord. One woman who ran a Post Office in Wales had an unseen helper, who tidied the shop for her every night. Being, no doubt, a truly wise Welshwoman,

11

this lady did not question what was happening, but just thanked the 'helper' out loud, each morning. She called 'him' Billy and he never once let her down, only leaving when she retired and had no further need for him.

Another account from Somerset reflects the beauty of the faery kingdom. In 1977 a lady, whom we may call C.M., was in her garden with her mother, who was showing her how to take cuttings from rose trees. She and her mother stood facing each other with the rose tree between them, when her mother put her finger to her lips and pointed to one of the flowers. 'With astonishment I saw what she was seeing – a little figure about 6 inches (15 centimetres) high, in the perfect shape of a woman and with brilliantly coloured diaphanous wings resembling those of a dragonfly. The figure held a little wand and was pointing it at the heart of a rose. At the tip of the wand there was a little light, like a star. The figure's limbs were a very pale pink and visible through her clothes. She had long silvery hair that resembled an aura. She hovered near the rose for at least two minutes, her wings vibrating rapidly like those of a humming-bird and then she disappeared.'

What surprised both the women was how like this figure was, in almost every respect, to the standard type of faery in children's stories. However, perhaps this is not so outstanding. We are apt to dismiss such mental pictures as 'mere imagination' forgetting how creative and insightful the imagination is. Far from 'dreaming up' the essentially impossible, we may see with the eye of imagination things which are invisible to the dense, physical eye. Besides, if faeries are creatures from another dimension or spiritual beings, we can only perceive them in ways we can understand. Globes of shining energy, which is what such beings may be, may be turned into human figures by the brain in order that we may perceive them meaningfully. Yet again, perhaps the faeries are appearing to us in the way they wish to be seen, and what could be more beautiful than the rose faery?

ROBERT KIRK

Living from 1644 to 1692, Robert Kirk, a Scottish minister, produced an important work on faery lore, called *The Secret Commonwealth of Elves, Fauns and Fairies*, which examines the beliefs of the Scottish Highlanders dispassionately but with a faith in their factual basis. Robert Kirk writes of many subjects that still live on in faery lore and are part of the experience of those who today have mystical experience of the Fair Folk, such as faery lovers, faery co-walkers, the gift of second sight and even some very holistic philosophies that seem to link his experiences of faeries with what many of us believe were the attitudes of our prehistoric forbears, such as the ever-repeating spiral of existence and the inter-dependence of life.

The body of Robert Kirk, clad only in his nightshirt, was found beside the Fairy Knowe at Aberfoyle, suggesting a sudden demise while taking a walk. However, the local people did not look at it quite that way. They said that the 'body' found was not the real corpse, but a 'stock' or faery substitute made to look like the real thing, while Kirk himself had been taken by the faeries because he had broadcast their secrets. After his 'death' Robert Kirk is said to have appeared to his cousin, Grahame of Duchray, saying that he was in fact a prisoner in Faerieland, but there was a single chance of escape. His posthumous child was due to be christened and if his cousin would keep his dirk handy at the service, ready to throw over the ghostly form of the erstwhile minister, he would be free to come home. When Kirk appeared Duchray was too surprised to do anything and so the chance was lost. Having experienced one ghostly encounter, is it not a little odd that the cousin was so surprised as to be immobile? The lore of faeries is full of such lost chances.

Not forever, perhaps. As recently as the Second World War there were still hopes of Kirk's release, for his chair stood in the dining-room and the story was that if anyone stuck a dirk into the seat of it, during a christening, he would be freed. An officer's pregnant wife who was tenant at the Manse in Aberfoyle, hoped that she would still be there when her child was born, in order to free Robert Kirk from his enslavement. However, it seems this was not tried after all and Kirk remains in bondage.

Thomas the Rhymer

Perhaps the most classic encounter from faery lore is that of Thomas Rymour of Erceldoune, also called Thomas the Rhymer and True Thomas. He was a real person who lived in Scotland in the thirteenth century, but his story, which has passed into folklore, has naturally been embroidered. The tale of Thomas has come down to us in two poems, the first is the 'Romance', which was written in the century after the death of Thomas, the second is the 'Ballad' which was first written in the nineteenth century. Of the two the earlier version, which may have been partly the work of Thomas himself, has more the ring of authenticity and symbolic power, harking back to the old Goddess religion and initiation into Her mysteries.

The story tells how the Queen of Elfland fell in love with him and kept him with her, having repeated intercourse with the (naturally enthusiastic) Thomas. This can be seen as an initiatory experience at the hands of the Goddess, for after their union she becomes ghastly and terrible to behold, signifying that in embracing the Goddess we depart from duality, accepting Her dark side as well as Her light. Obviously a wise man, Thomas does not recoil from the Dark Mother. In so doing he faces his own dark side and becomes complete. The Dark Goddess is a destroyer, but this is simply in order to create anew and, in time, his Lady is restored to his sight in her former beauty. This tale is a mirror-image (as is so much of Faerieland) of the Arthurian tale of the ugly wife, wed by Gawain who, by virtue of his acceptance, turns back again to the beautiful maid she is in truth. Gawain is a champion of the Goddess and the Earth Mother and Thomas the Rhymer is also married to the sacred land. The Queen of Elfland is none other than the Goddess Herself. These are themes we shall be looking at in the following chapter 'Faeries and Magic'.

The Queen of Elfland carried Thomas away into the land of Faerie for seven years, releasing him only when the time for the tribute the faeries had to render to the Devil was due and she feared Thomas would be chosen. The story of Thomas was put to paper in times when the theological climate was more dogmatic. For those of us who do not believe in the Devil, we may take this 'tribute' as having

something to do with an initiatory or evolutionary step that it was not yet Thomas's time to take. Thomas is released back into the human realm, with the gift of a tongue that cannot lie. He proceeds to become an awesome seer, with seemingly magical abilities. Famous throughout Scotland for his powers, he foretold the union of Scotland and England 'in the ninth degree of the blood of Robert the Bruce' three centuries before it came to pass. However, the heart of Thomas belonged to Faerie and, at length, it reclaimed him. For while he was feasting with friends, many years after his return from Elfland, a messenger ran in, in great alarm, to tell the company that a hart and a hind had come out of the forest and were walking openly up the street.Without a word, Thomas rose from the table and followed the creatures back into the trees, never more to be seen.

The first encounter of Thomas with the Faerie Queen occurred under the Eildon Tree, which was a hawthorn, growing by the eerie Eildon Hills. The hawthorn is known as a tree of Faerieland. While this specific tree no longer stands, its site is yet marked by a stone. The hind may be taken as a representative of the Goddess in Her Maiden aspect and, indeed, all horned animals have powerful associations with the Old Religion, the pagan faith in Celtic and other countries. Thomas himself may have passed from this world, but he is still encountered by many who make journeys into Faerieland. Hugh Mynne, author of *The Faerie Way* (see Further Reading), describes him as a great guide and helper and has held meetings with him on the subtle planes.

'A.E.' The Seer

'A.E.' was the pen-name of an Irishman called George William Russell, who was born in the mid-nineteenth century. Besides being a poet and possessing 'the sight' he was an eminently practical and educated individual, a journalist and editor with especial talent in economics and rural agriculture. He has left many very detailed accounts of his visions, both in descriptive prose and in stunning mystical pictures. A.E. was quite clear that the faeries were the

shining races of the Sidhe, living in the Celtic Otherworld. He makes a distinction between certain Shining Beings and Opalescent Beings, the former being more of the 'group soul' type, without individualized life, whereas the Opalescent faeries draw energy from the Earth's subtle essence and are much greater and more spiritual, sometimes emitting elemental entities from themselves, which they later receive back within.

The Shining Beings A.E. describes as being of a similar height to ours, while the Opalescent Beings are about 4.5 metres (14 feet) in height. This is an interesting figure. In his book *Nothing In This Book is True, But It's Exactly How Things Are* (Frog Ltd. Books, 1994) Bob Frissell describes five levels of consciousness associated with our planet, which are related to the number of chromosomes and to height. Level One corresponds to the Aborigines and the Dreamtime. Here, there is an experience of 'oneness'. There are 42 plus 2 chromosomes and a height of 1 to 1.5 metres (3.5 to 5 feet). The second level, where we are now, is one of discord, but such is necessary in order to make transition and advance. We have 44 plus 2 chromosomes and our height range is between 1.5 and 2 metres (5 and 7 feet). The third level of consciousness Frissell equated with Christ consciousness, where there are 46 plus 2 chromosomes and a height range between 3 and 5 metres (10 and 16 feet). Here, there is once more a unity consciousness, at a higher level, where what is thought and remembered is remembered by all and manifests instantly. The following two levels need not concern us. What is striking is the alignment between the height of Frissell's third level and A.E.'s Opalescent Beings. Frissell's book is about our emergence into a new consciousness and a new dimension. The great ones of the Sidhe quite probably already inhabit that dimension.

A.E. is an important figure in regard to the tradition of faeries because he was able to frame his experiences in ways that were acceptable and inspiring to the thinkers of his day, so adding an important dimension to the old faery lore. A.E. was aware of the presence of the Great Mother Goddess as the Irish goddess Dana, who gave her name to the Tuatha de Danaan. From her all things emanate and she is at once the great Goddess of the Sidhe, the basis for all material form and Divine Compassion itself.

The Cottingley Fairies

From the sublime visions of the mystic we come down to the realm of hoax, cliché fairies, tiny beings, with wings, created from cardboard cut-outs and used in deceptive photographs. But this may not be a fair description.

In 1917 Frances Griffiths and Elsie Wright, two cousins living in Cottingley, West Yorkshire, claimed to have seen fairies. In 1920 the Christmas issue of the *Strand* magazine printed an article by Sir Arthur Conan Doyle concerning the photographs of fairies taken by the two girls. Opinion was divided. Sceptics were amused and scathing, but many people, among them several eminent thinkers, were convinced of the existence of nature spirits.

The affair remained a mystery until the 1980s when the girls, both by now old ladies, admitted that they had faked four out of the five photos. Doubters could now assume a smug grin, with an 'I told you so'. Opinion holds that the last photo also looks faked and, as the others were, why should this one be genuine? Elsie confirmed in the 1980s that she had never believed in fairies, but the same is not true of Frances. Frances was an efficient and highly effectual woman who was matron at a boys' school, with a reputation for being blisteringly straight. Her daughter said of her after her death that she could not tell a lie if she tried.

The Cottingley case has been described very fully in a book by Joe Cooper (see Further Reading) and has formed the basis for the film *Fairy Story*. Like many such cases it remains inconclusive. Those who scoff at the notion of faeries will consider the case, if case there ever was, to be proven. Others may admit the possibility of doubt. Psychic ability, self-delusion and desire for attention can get mixed up and many reports and instances of the paranormal are extremely elusive when it comes to anything like 'proof'. However, the smoke is far too dense for there to be no fire at all. People who 'see things' are themselves often doubtful, embarrassed and confused. When one is not believed there is always the temptation to fake evidence. If there ever were faeries in the beck at Cottingley, presumably they are still there.

ELEMENTS IN TRADITIONAL ENCOUNTERS

Evans Wentz (see Further Reading) compiled a vast body of anecdotal evidence regarding interactions with faeries, drawn from Ireland, Scotland, Wales, Cornwall, the Isle of Man and Brittany. It is only relatively recently that the existence of faeries has been rejected by ordinary people. Evans Wentz, interviewing at the turn of the twentieth century, was able to catch the tail end of what had once been a universal belief, reportedly inherited by peasants from an ancient, cultured class.

It seems that the character of faeries varies with the terrain. On the west coast of Ireland the tradition is the most vigorous and faeries are most easily seen. The Irish faeries are generally of a more gentle disposition than those in Scotland, where the country is more harsh. The belief existed that the 'good people' can see everything and that they are immensely powerful, for some of them could destroy half the world, if they so chose, but they do not. They take on all forms, big and little. If they are seen as small this does not mean they are small 'in reality'. They live in 'raths' or faery forts which are underground or, sometimes, at the bottom of a lake. Often they go in procession and even more frequently they dance. It is a grievous offence to violate a faery preserve and tales abound of the misfortune which has come to pass on those who have trespassed. Similarly, one must not build over a faery track.

These creatures may take the young, beautiful and intellectually or artistically gifted and they take them body and soul. Often faeries can only be seen with one eye and there are accounts of faeries, when they realize they are being spied upon, causing blindness in the offending eye, or both, or blowing upon the eyes, from which time the subject can see faeries no longer. The ability to see faeries can be transmitted, at least temporarily, by touch when a seer, observing the Fair Folk, touches his partner with his foot and, while the contact is in place, the companion can see them too. Tir Na Nog, the Irish Otherworld, where retreated the Tuatha de Danaan

after their defeat by the Milesians, is described by A.E. as 'a radiant archetype of this world' replete with harmony and beauty, but there are other places where horrible things may be perceived. Sometimes children are born that are hybrids of human and faery and they may need ointment placed upon their eyes to enable them to see as one of Faerieland. There are many tales of human midwives brought to help faery births. If the ointment should find its way into the eyes of the midwife, she too can see faeries and their land and, because of this, there are stories of the blinding of midwives by the faeries.

Faeries have been reported to endow clairvoyance, taking people across the world in a twinkling to observe events, hundreds of miles away, that were later verified. People who enter a state of trance for some while, or for several days, may be assumed to be communing with the faeries. Some who returned from such interludes denied ever seeing the Fair Folk, and this may be because they forgot, or because they were told to say nothing. These people may be spotted holding secret communion with faeries, but on the other hand, the faeries are likely to sense the unwanted presence and stay away. Faery paths, that run from nowhere to nowhere, are in fact paths between the realms. There are various taboos that operate in relation to faeries, for instance the aforesaid violation of faery preserves, where no tree or stone must be disturbed. More specifically, there is a taboo on the cutting of any crops after Samhain (31 October) on pain of attracting the unwelcome attentions of the pooka, a horrid black goblin that often appeared as a hideous black horse. Contacts may also be made with the faeries and once a bargain is made it must be kept. Simple ways of propitiating faeries might be to leave out an offering of milk or food. However, if a more specific gift is required of faeries, they may strike a hard bargain indeed.

From these snippets it may be deduced that the world of Faerie is tricky and dangerous, as well as wondrous. The point about 'price' rather troubled me, as my sense is that gifts on the subtle planes are given freely. I discussed this with a female friend, who is experienced in the occult, and she said she had observed that men were often treated more harshly in these matters, because their approach tends to be more adversarial, with attitudes that may be allied to command,

hierarchy and possession, whereas the feminine way is possibly more co-operative. We make offerings and we would not ask for something for nothing. Make of this what you will. Faerie encounters, at least superficially, are not always characterized by what we might regard as ordinary morality.

SUMMING UP

The above is just a tiny extract from the vast heritage of faery lore and a myriad encounters with them. While one or several of the possible categories of 'faery' given at the start of the chapter might be applicable to each case, this is my attitude to faeries. I regard them as objectively real as my friends and family, although of a different order of 'reality' and while I do think that psychological interpretations are often valid and meaningful, I do not see them as the full story. I feel they are inhabitants of another dimension, vibrational level, the 'astral plane' or Otherworld. These terms are possibly totally interchangeable, but I believe that there are varying levels or frequencies of Otherworld. 'Faeries' may not be all on the same frequency but I would guess they mostly are and that it is a frequency close, in some way, to our own and, having meaningful interaction with it, often forming something of a mirror image. The seemingly meaningless or mischievous antics of faeries may be because of our limited perceptions, or because they are trying to 'shock' us in some way. Some faeries might be as put out to see us as we are to see them!

These Otherworld beings no doubt come in several varieties. For instance, there are accounts of nature spirits and these seem to operate in a hierarchy. The 'higher' nature spirits may be called devas or equated with angels. The traditional type of tiny, winged creature may be a guise of the basic nature spirit and these care for specific sections of the natural world and plants. In addition there are the elementals, which express the energy of the forms of the natural world. Above and beyond there are the beings I, and others, call the people of the Sidhe, told about in Irish mythology, and these mysterious and powerful entities can be an inspiration to us, mediating the Divine, although

the Goddess Herself lies within and beyond all manifestation. In some respects all types of faery are an expression of the life and divinity that exists within all of the material world. Because faeries are within Otherworld, I see no reason why we should not be with them when we die, at least for some time and in some places. So faeries may indeed, at times, be equated with the souls of the dead.

PRACTICE

FAERY RESEARCH

Accounts of faeries and similar entities are encountered around the World. The lore is extremely rich in Celtic countries, especially Ireland and, most of all, its hauntingly beautiful western coast. Accounts of faeries are legion in the old Celtic strongholds of Scotland, Wales, Cornwall, the Isle of Man and Brittany. However, the Native Americans also have a powerful Otherworld tradition, as do the Aborigines of Australia.

If you wish to research faeries you may like to start with your own family heritage. Your family tree may reveal some Celtic ancestry, generations back. What accounts have been passed down? Did anyone ever report seeing a leprechaun, hearing the banshee, fleeing from a water kelpie or living in dread of the Twlwyth Teg? Has anyone ever had a spirit helper? Bear in mind that many people are very reluctant to speak of such things for fear of being considered silly and that for every person who embroiders their experience there are, quite probably, several who suppress it.

Enquire also in your locality. Books on history and folklore can be found in your library and many large bookshops feature a section on local subjects and local authors. If you are fairly extravert and have a talent for starting up conversations with strangers, some of the old locals may well have a tale or two to tell. If you live in a city there is unlikely to be quite the same material, so you may have to go further afield.

It is fairly well accepted that some places are exceptionally susceptible to paranormal happenings. These may involve lines of 'energy' on, or just below, the surface of the earth. Many people believe there are a variety of such lines, while others discount their existence. However, it does seem to many of us that certain places are very 'powerful' and if we find ourselves resorting to New Age clichés, that is possibly due to the inadequacies of the language. Places of power include sites of stone circles, standing stones, barrow mounds and the like. Sites held sacred in Native American and Australian Aboriginal tradition are, by all accounts, similar. There is usually a considerable body of legend attached to the more notable sites. You may like to visit, to soak up the atmosphere and find out as much as you can.

FAERIES AND MAGIC

Over hill, over dale,
Thorough bush, thorough brier,
Over park, over pale,
Thorough flood, thorough fire

W. Shakespeare, *A Midsummer Night's Dream*

Whatever you think faeries are and however you regard them, they are the very stuff of magic. Magic, of course, is as contentious a subject as faeries themselves! However, those who work magic know that it is about moving among the subtle realms of which faeries themselves are a part, because magic involves a shift in consciousness. Magic is the art of making real changes, through an act of will. It is also about belief and imagination and, although simple, it is also mysterious, for spells weave themselves first in the land of Faerie and magic takes place at the interface between subjective and objective reality. Magic changes the person who works it.

FAERIES AND THE OLD RELIGION

Before the advent of Christianity, the British Isles were pagan. Until recently the word 'pagan' had come to be synonymous with the barbarous and backward, but paganism, in many forms, is currently enjoying a revival. Pagan faiths honour Mother Earth and all of the natural world, seeing divinity within all that exists. To most pagans the sense of Otherworld is very real, such as it was to the Celtic people from whom many of our ideas about faeries derive. Three

aspects of paganism are animism, pantheism and polytheism. Animism means that everything is alive, including rocks, crystals, etc. This outlook has been labelled 'primitive' but it is arguably the greatest form of spirituality, to see life in all things and to feel that deity exists within all, which is the meaning of pantheism. Polytheism means there are many gods and goddesses.

To all of these approaches the belief in faeries is highly relevant, for faeries are many and varied. The more 'basic' faery, or elemental or nature spirit, may be thought of as the living breath of the land and they are a testimony to the fact that deity is everywhere, while the more differentiated order of faery may be equated with the old gods and goddesses, especially the Celtic ones, which are inseparable from the faery tradition. However, we can also be sure that the tradition of faeries is far older than Celtic culture. It is widely accepted that neolithic culture was matrifocal, that is centred around influential females, and that the power of the feminine was vibrantly felt. Essential to Goddess worship, both ancient and modern, is a sense of the 'indwellingness' of spirit, the sacredness of the material world and of everyday life. Rather than a separate, theoretical heaven existing beyond the 'dense' world of matter, paradise is close at hand and the dimensions of Otherworld are entwined with our own. Along with Goddess worship goes an interest in opening our inner sight and finding our own path, which brings us into the realms of magic.

Hugh Mynne (see Further Reading) has this to say:

> Faerieland is a parallel dimension, coexisting with our own. We are intimately connected to it by the luminous fibers radiating from our light bodies. In many aspects, it is an energy counterpart of the physical earth, with the light fibers acting as a means of transmission of energy between the two, like high-powered electric cables. But there are many animals and beings unique to Faerieland ...

> It is probable that much of the Faerie symbology derives ultimately from the Neolithic period of prehistory ... a predominately peaceful one ... The importance of the Goddess to the Faerie Way cannot be overstated, and seems to be a direct inheritance from the Neolithic past.

While there are male faeries, it would seem that what we usually think of as female energy is more usually manifested in these rarified creatures. They are a testimony to the varied nature of creation, the closeness of the subtle planes, showing us that there are indeed other dimensions besides our own, opening us to the ways of magic and to the powers of our own inner sight. Witchcraft, best described as 'Wise-craft', is a type of paganism very much concerned with worship of the Goddess and the natural world, emphasizing inner 'knowingness'. (Of course, witchcraft is nothing to do with worshipping the devil, in whom witches do not believe, nor is it about anything remotely 'evil'. Witchcraft is fully described in *Witchcraft – A Beginner's Guide* in this series.) A specific tradition of witchcraft is called The Faerie Tradition, founded by Victor Anderson, after his initiatory encounter with a strange and magical old woman, who opened his eyes in a mystical vision of the Goddess and the Horned God of nature. This tradition is the same as Hugh Mynne's 'Faerie Way' and rests, like all witchcraft approaches, on the insight into the Universe as a web of energy, revealed to shamans of the Stone Age as it is revealed in modern times to those who wish to see. The writer Starhawk is an initiate of this tradition and her work *The Spiral Dance* (Harper and Row, 1979) is a classic on the subject.

The magic circle

Magical work is undertaken inside a magic circle, that the practitioner casts at the start of the ritual. This circle is composed of etheric energy, which emanates from the person casting the circle. This 'energy' is around and within us all the time and within all of the manifest world but it is gathered and focused by an act of will and imagination. Thus a magic circle is in place if you strongly visualize it. The more often you do it the better you are likely to get at it and proper tools and rituals make the whole business easier, more dramatic and more effectual. Faeries and the creatures of Otherworld are able to see or sense this circle.

The purposes of the circle are several and many people feel that its principal function is to contain the energies raised in the ritual until the correct time when they can be consciously sent to the task in hand. Another use of the circle is protection, so that no stray entities may come too close and cause trouble, because magical working, if it is strong, is akin to lighting a beacon in the astral world, of which faeries are a part. The circle is also a 'half-way house' between this world and Otherworld, so helping the shifts in consciousness that take place. Forming the magic circle is explained in *Witchcraft – A Beginner's Guide* in this series published by Hodder & Stoughton.

After the circle has been cast and cleansed, the next step is to call on the 'Guardians'. These Guardians have different names in different traditions. They are also called 'watchtowers', 'elemental powers', 'the directions' and they were even called 'the corners' in the film *The Craft* although I do not know from which tradition, if any, that term was culled! However, it all boils down to the same thing, for what we are calling on here is a specific and very powerful type of energy from the Faerie realms.

Elements and elementals

The four elements are very important in magic and also in astrology, for they represent four different types of the material state, four different types of attitude, four different types of energy and, as such, they are very basic and potent in the magical outlook. A symbol that relates to the four elements in the magic circle is the Celtic cross, which is really a symbol of the magic circle itself. The equal-armed cross is far older than Christianity and signifies balance and developed awareness on the material plane. Thus it is also a protective symbol.

The number four is a number of manifestation and solidity. A table on four legs balances nicely. There are four dimensions to our reality – height, length, breadth and time, through which we are seen to move.

The four directions of East, South, West and North give us our earthly co-ordinates. Calling on these earths us and is a statement of our intent as well as a protection and a source of power.

Each of the directions equates with an element and, while there are variations on this, especially among the various traditions of the Native Americans, these are the associations that I, and many others, feel are the most basic and time-honoured. They are North/Earth, East/Air, South/Fire, West/Water. Understandably, many people in the Southern Hemisphere like to shift these associations, because for you South is the direction of cold and darkness, better linked to Earth than to Fire, and North takes you closer to the Sun and heat.

The element of Earth

After the circle has been cast and cleansed, it is the time to invoke the elemental guardians. It is usual to start with Earth, in the North, for Earth is the element that is basic to our survival, our grounding, and it is from the Earth that we have sprung, and to which we shall all return, until the time that we are reborn, again upon Earth. Earth equates to molecules in their cold and least excitable state. From a psychological point of view it is about practicality, common sense, what is workable, solid and reliable. The astrological signs related to this element are Taurus, Virgo and Capricorn.

So, for those of us in the Northern Hemisphere, we stand in the centre of the circle, facing North, the 'blind' side of the sky, where the lights of Sun and Moon never pass, to call upon the elemental King and Queen of the North, the powers of Earth. Those of us who do this are not always very clear about what we are, in fact, doing until we have to think about it and explain. For me what happens is that a kind of 'rip' is created in reality as we know it. At our summoning, the elemental King and Queen are present and visible to our inner sight. The Queen I see as the presiding essence of the element, while the King is its driving force. With, around and coming from these beings, forces or however you wish to conceive them, are the faery hosts of that element. These beings are also called 'elementals' and

the elementals of Earth are called 'gnomes'. Thus we are inviting these forces to be present in a very real way, to give power and protection, and we might specifically call on one species of elemental to help us in a selected endeavour. For instance, if our working was about the creation of a beautiful garden, we would understandably ask for the help of the gnomes to bring this about.

Several points need to be made here. I do not feel that the gnomes are precisely the same as the 'nature spirits' that are more fully explored elsewhere. The gnomes are about the power of elemental Earth, and as such one of the factors involved in plant growth, ore, gems, crystals, etc. but they are not quite the same as the nature spirits that tend plants, flowers and trees. I also want to comment on the word 'summon' used in respect of the elements. This is an appropriate word in some respects, for we need to be very definite and focused, so that we send out a very clear call. I believe that the elemental monarchs are glad to help, for anything that fosters understanding between humans and the spirit world and that draws us closer to the world of nature is welcomed by them. Also, time being different in their world, from our perspective they have plenty of it! However, to imagine that we can command these beings is a mistake, for they are more powerful and more far-seeing than we are, and they come because they want to, albeit our sense of urgency is not lost on them. The elements must always be thanked, before they depart. As we summon them, we honour them and delight in them, for their purity and brilliance is unearthly, to the point where it brings tears to the eyes. I find this is especially the case with elemental Water. The elements are always brought into the circle, quite literally, water in a chalice, earth as a stone or a pentagram (five-point star) engraved on a disk, fire as candle-flame and air as incense. Certain symbols also designate the elements, for instance the ritual knife or athame equates with air and the cutting edge and focus of the intellect, while the wand or staff is linked with fire. However, it is well known that faeries do not like iron and, for this reason, some traditions do not allow anything metal in the circle. Thus your choice of athame would need to be one made from flint, or wood. This may relate to the relationship between the faeries and the people of pre-Iron Age civilization, to their dislike of the despoiling of the Earth, necessary to extract iron or, perhaps,

29

because metal, being a good conductor of electricity, disrupts their subtle energy patterns. To find out more about rituals for summoning the elements and about tools, such as the athame, please consult *Witchcraft – A Beginner's Guide* as mentioned above.

The gnomes can be grumpy and reserved, industrious and very close guardians of Mother Earth and her resources. You can make friends with gnomes, nature spirits and many other types of faery by showing respect for the Earth and by doing your bit to look after a plot of soil. Ask the help of the gnomes for anything practical – gardening, craftwork, building an extension or anything solid. You do not have to see them, or even believe in them, for them to help you (although I believe all faeries can have churlish and mischievous moods, especially with those who will not entertain the possibility of their existence – and, please note, that is not the same as the healthy scepticism of intelligence but, rather, the closed mind of bigotry). Go out and touch solid rock, or place your hands in the soil, or even sit in a cave, and imagine the presence of the gnomes. Frame your request clearly and ask for their help. Pledge a gift in return and thank them in anticipation.

The element of Air

As we travel deosil, i.e. 'sunwise' around our circle, from the North, the next direction at which we arrive is East. Sunwise, in the Northern Hemisphere is clockwise and, in the Southern Hemisphere, it is anti-clockwise. For those of you in the Southern Hemisphere, if you equate South with Earth, your sunwise movement will bring you to East.

East is the direction of sunrise, connected to the time of day when we awaken out of our unconscious slumber, coming into the clarity of thought, the ability to reflect. It is the direction associated with the element of Air. Gaseous molecules are at their most free moving, swiftest and lightest. Most gases are quite invisible and yet they can seep into all but the most carefully sealed places. Like thought they move with great speed, but they can be seen only by their

manifestation, as the trees bend in the wind. So, psychologically, the element of Air relates to our ability to think, to analyse, to be detached and reflective, not so that we may be stranded in some arid intellectual desert, but so we may understand, feel free and find inspiration. The astrological signs Gemini, Libra and Aquarius are Air signs, and the Air elementals are called *sylphs*.

The sylphs can help us in any matter where we seek to become detached, to see the whole picture as a bird on the wing sees the panorama of hill, valley, wood and field, and is not blinded by what is under its beak. Sylphs can cleanse and clarify, freeing the mind of its cobwebs and so open the way to the true power of the liberated spirit. The sylphs aren't all that keen on sacred cows. Nor do they appreciate pollution of their sphere by smoke and gases that affect the atmosphere. You could call on the help of the sylphs for a coming exam, or an interview, where you need to keep your mind sharp and clear, or for some problem where you feel you are 'missing something'. Naturally, you will feel closest to the sylphs if you can climb up to the top of a hill, where the air is fresh. Breathe deeply and call on these ethereal beings. Do not forget to promise a gift in return.

The element of fire

Our deosil journey now brings us to the South and the realm of Fire. When a substance is on fire its molecules are in a state of great excitement and transformation. Fire can eat up and destroy, it can cleanse and purify, it can throw 'new light' on a situation and it provides warmth, cheer and a raising of the spirits. Fire is very exciting. Those of us who live in cold climates are drawn to warm places, which we see as the home of passion, vibrancy and inspiration. In the Northern Hemisphere, the fiery wheel of the Sun is in the South, where it burns high and strong at midday, and for the Southern Hemisphere the same is true of the North. At the depths of a bonfire there shines a magical world – this is the world of the *salamanders*, or fire spirits. Making 'fire pictures' is an act of drawing closer to the salamanders and, if we are lucky, we may catch a glimpse of them in their ethereal dance within the flames.

Fire relates to inspiration and to vision that is beyond the here and now, not by any means necessarily in a 'psychic' fashion, but to the act of projecting consciousness into the future, going beyond boundaries (as a firework may do) and to unpredictable places, to stimulate the imagination and to be creative. It is an element of energy in its purest form. The Fire signs are Aries, Leo and Sagittarius.

You may like to call on the salamanders for help when you need some extra sparkle, for warmth, *joie de vivre*, courage and, of course, inspiration. By merely lighting a candle you are inviting their presence. The salamanders can give you a helping of pizzazz, such as when you are about to appear on stage, give a talk, or if you are attempting anything which, for you, is challenging. They can also show some amazing perspectives, not necessarily with the breadth of the sylphs, but with greater inspiration, where the impossible may be seen to be possible, from some quirky angle. In these days of microwaves and central heating, fire is not often seen in our lives, and we are the poorer for it, so a simple gift to the salamanders can be the lighting of a suitable fire such as a candle. The flames of inspiration are also, I believe, pleasing to the salamanders.

The element of Water

In our deosil rotation we come finally to the West and to Water. We know that molecules in their liquid state are at once fluid but accessible to the senses. We can feel water, identify it, contain it in a bowl, immerse ourselves in it, and yet water runs off us, runs from between our cupped fingers and escapes from bowl or bucket, when this is overset, running away into cracks and crannies, never more to be gathered. Water exists in a special relationship to life on Earth, for our bodies are about 75 per cent water, as the globe of the Earth is covered, in similar proportion, by the oceans. As the Sun goes down in the West, so creeps in the time of enchantment, when our logical minds lose their hold and our daily routines and demands are put to one side in favour of family, friends, socializing, the bonds of love and love-making itself. It is a time when we may read, watch

35

television or escape into fantasy in preparation for sleep. Water is the element that relates to the emotions, to tradition, community, feeling and love. The Water signs are Cancer, Scorpio and Pisces and the Water elementals are called the *undines*.

The undines are graceful and beautiful, for the most part, but they may be allied to more terrifying creatures such as the Water Kelpie, which appears as a young horse, lures riders inescapably on to his back and takes them down into the river's depths and drowns them, or the Water Wraith, a dreadful scowling female who lures or drags travellers under the surface to a watery demise. Psychologically this relates to the 'waters' of the unconscious overwhelming the conscious mind. The undines may be a little put out by the fact that we devalue the world of dreams, our roots and ancestry in favour of what we are pleased to call 'progress' and the 'rational'. However, they are gentle beings with a love of music and beauty. We are all familiar with the traditional mermaid and her enchanting singing, although undines may be of either sex or no sex at all.

The undines can help you to cleanse your heart, to find consolation in sorrow and to find love, especially to open out to a deep love of nature and the love that is waiting there in return. They may help with family matters and in gaining an instinctual wisdom and understanding. Naturally you can draw close to the undines near rivers, lakes and the ocean. A gift in return could be some act of cleansing of waterways, even if it just pulling some weeds out of a choked pond.

The faerie cities

The Faerie tradition describes the four cities of the Faerie realm. Hugh Mynne (see Further Reading) defines these as 'node points of the wisdom-energy of the elements'. We can visit these cities in inward journeys, that can also be regarded as the most 'outward' journey we could ever take, because we are going out of our ordinary physical confines into Otherworld. As we do so we are forging links and creating a magic circle that involves both ourselves and the outside world in a system of wholeness and we strengthen our

connection to the subtle world and its energy points. Such spirit journeys are, to a great extent, under our own direction and not the same as the experiences of those who report being taken bodily into the land of Faerie. These journeys, and the totality of the faery path, are described by Hugh Mynne in his beautiful book *The Faerie Way*, which is a working guidebook of the Faerie realms. For now, let us look briefly at the Faerie cities, to make more vivid our appreciation of the elements.

Each of these cities corresponds to one of the four elements, Earth, Fire, Air and Water and, when we invoke these at the four quarters of our circle, we are opening a doorway into each of the cities, making available to us the particular strength, energy and wisdom of the Faerie city. The following are brief descriptions, not instructions for an inward journey, for which you will need to consult Hugh Mynne.

GORIAS

Gorias is the city of the East. Here, in an emerald valley, runs a mountain stream, fed by many crystal cascades from the high rocks. Many square white buildings cling to the sides of the surrounding mountains, flying pennants from their roofs that flutter in the fresh breeze. Further up the valley is a cubical building with a shining golden roof. On the approach to this building are many cheerful people, working in the fields. The valley is beautiful, resplendent with brilliant flowers, with an atmosphere of peace and industriousness.

Within the gold-roofed building there are many gorgeous hangings, depicting varieties of mythical creatures, terrible, beautiful and magical. Situated in a dimly-lit, further room is a statue of pure gold, illuminating the room with its radiance. It is a man with a drawn sword in his right hand and a flower in his left. This is a most beautiful and touching image of the 'unsheathed' intellect accompanied by gentleness and of what we might term a 'masculine' potency that is balanced by the value of the 'feminine'. The faery teacher who inhabits Gorias is called *Esras*.

FINIAS

Finias is the city of the South. Here, there is a cluster of ancient buildings, in an oasis in the middle of the desert sands. A huge archway straddles a road that heads out into the desert, only to dissolve and disappear in the arid landscape. The arch is covered with arcane symbols and the city itself is composed of adobe huts, interspersed with silvery trees. The inhabitants of the place are cordial. This is a place of eternal light, where night never falls. The desert road leads into the city, under the arch and towards a large edifice built from huge stones but which is in a state of disrepair.

Inside this building it is cool and dim and on the earthen floor is engraved a spiral. Here the urge is to dance, to become one with the web of creation. In another room, without windows, is a wooden staff, planted in the middle of the floor. This staff spontaneously grows branches and blossoms as you watch. A subtle scent permeates and the gift of eternal light seems available. Both Finias and Gorias offer gentle, highly potent images. The faery teacher of Finias is called *Uiscias*.

MURIAS

Murias is the city of the West. It lies between low hills, on the shores of a western ocean. The Sun is setting below the waves and rain drops are blown on the wind, making the cobbles of Murias glisten, and causing the tradespeople to bustle about, bringing their goods under cover. Many ships stand in the harbour and trees, resplendent in shades of autumn, intersperse the red-tiled roofs of the houses.

A little path leads up towards the western door of a great cathedral. Inside it is dimly lit, with many strange carvings speaking of Otherworld wisdom. At the eastern end is a splendid rose window, barely lit by the rays of the dying Sun. Wonderfully, this window is suddenly afire with light and seems to be blossoming like a real rose. Light and blossom also unfold within your heart. Upon the altar there is a golden chalice, perfect in form. The faery teacher of Murias is called *Semias*.

Falias

Falias is the city of the North, approached through thick darkness. The metallic towers of Falias are topped by brilliant crystals, that glow steadily, like beacons. Falias is a massive and impressive city, as if it is a blueprint for all the cities on Earth. There are no people, no cars, no animals, but something about this place is deeply alive. Its broad streets are strangely familiar.

In the middle of the city stands a block of meteoric rock, ancient as the Earth itself. There is an aura of light playing about this stone and with it an endless stream of memories, both personal and collective, of this world and other worlds, making you conscious of your innumerable lifetimes and the depthless wisdom of Falias. Touching this rock opens you to the ancientness of your own soul. The fairy teacher of Falias is *Morfesa*.

These descriptions make some aspects of the Faerie kingdom more vivid, indicating how it can impact upon our awareness. Naturally, to make real use of them and to experience them personally, you will need to embark upon the path of the mysteries and the craft of the wise.

Faery spells

There are many ways that we can use to draw close to the faeries, either simply because we want to, or to enlist their help in a matter. Faeries are also believed to have links with certain trees and plants. Here is a selection of faery charms.

FOR DISCOVERING TREE-SPIRITS

This is a charm given by Valerie Worth in *The Crone's Book of Words*, Llewellyn, 1994.

When the moon is round
In spring or summer
Go to a place
Where more than two
But not over twenty
Trees are growing,
Measure their bounds
By silent walking,
Mark their centre
And in it stand
But make no sound;
Listen and watch
And you may find
Green and silver
Shadows flying
From leaf to leaf,
And a noise like water
Or quiet talking;
Strike three times
With a stick of oak
Upon the ground –
Then you may see
In every tree
The falling streams
Of their silver hair,
And their hands
Like silver-flickering air;
Their frightened emerald
Eyes will stare
Until you look away –
Then though you stay
For a year and a day,
You will not see them again.

FAERIES AND NATURE SPIRITS – A BEGINNER'S GUIDE

PSYCHIC BREW

Brew up a psychic tea to drink, prior to a midnight walk in the full
Moon, to see the Fair Folk. Use spring water, rain-water (but not
where pollution is strong) or filtered tap-water for the brew. Use flame
to make your brew if you can (please don't use the microwave) and
avoid metal containers. Assemble your herbs, grind them manually
with pestle and mortar, mix them and place about a handful in a pot,
preferably a special pot, acquired for the purpose. Close your eyes
and visualize your intent, which is to see faeries. Hold your open
palms over the herbs in the pot and visualize your energies going into
the herbs in a stream of golden light, while you still affirm your intent
to see the Fair Folk. Pull your hands back close to your body and
take a deep breath, gathering your energy back inside you. Now pour
two cups of boiling water on to the herbs and cover the pot with a
lid. Leave for 13 minutes, for 13 is a magical number. Strain without
using a metal strainer – cheesecloth may be best, as plastic isn't
favoured either. Drink a cup before seeking your encounter and
return what you do not use to the Earth.

This recipe is given by Scott Cunningham in *The Complete Book of
Incense, Oils and Brews*, Llewellyn, 1991. It consists of:

    3 parts rose petals
    2 parts yarrow
    1 part cinnamon

Ideally you should grow these plants yourself and gather the
ingredients by the light of the Moon, as she waxes to full, but I am
sure if you buy them, especially from a supplier who prides
themselves on the purity of their ingredients for magical purposes,
this will be fine.

Another concoction given by Scott Cunningham, for clairvoyance,
has the following ingredients:

    3 parts rose petals
    1 part cinnamon
    1 part nutmeg
    1 part bay
    1 part mugwort

42

This one would be more 'pokey'. After steeping the ingredients in boiling water, sniff the steam, visualizing its psychic power permeating your whole being. You could sip just a little, also, prior to your search for the faeries.

INCENSE

Incense alters the psychic atmosphere and speaks directly to 'Younger Self' which is the term the writer Starhawk coined for our instinctual side, which is both playful and deeply wise. Lots of different incenses can be bought in New Age shops and centres. You will need a suitable, tough, container for your incense and some charcoal. Light the side of the charcoal 'wheel' while holding it in tongs. When it sparks, it has ignited, so hold it for a while to let the burning get established, then put down the charcoal disk and sprinkle incense in the little dip in the middle. If you are very psychic you may begin to see spirits at once, in the smoke! Always affirm to yourself your intent, beforehand. Burn your incense and allow a dreamy state of mind to take over. For your incense you can use a blend of frankincense, bay and wormwood. Wormwood, however, smells very pungent, so I would generally use a preponderance of frankincense. You could burn this incense prior to visiting faery haunts or use it outdoors where you feel they are to be found. Remember to avoid metal containers near faeries.

FAERY HERBS

Faeries are connected to everything that lives and I am sure that each and every plant has its own faery guardian. However, there are certain herbs and flowers that are said to have especial affinity with the Fair Folk. It is also said by some that nettles deter faeries, but while I was hauling these out of the ground, with gloved hands, a voice inside my head said, 'What about nettle soup, then?' After that I felt sure that nettles also have their own type of faery and I don't see why others should be kept away. It is worth bearing in mind that when we ingest a plant we are partaking of its subtle essence, not just its nutritional value, and are thus potentially partaking of the related faery essence. Drugs made from plant

extracts connect the person who takes them with the spirit of the plant and can give a profound experience of the spirit world in shamanic journey. However, such drugs are no less dangerous than man-made chemical substances and may be more so.

PEONY ROOTS OR SEEDS

These can be made into a necklace and hung around the neck of a child as protection against faeries. It is well known that the faeries may be jealous of the beautiful and the wise. They may also fall in love with them …

PRIMROSES

I believe that the faeries love a primrose-studded bank, in spring, when the midday sunshine falls gently or fragrant dusk steals in. Growing blue and red primroses in the garden is said to attract faeries.

ROSES

These gorgeous flowers attract faeries. I feel that the dog-rose, *Rosa canina*, although not so beautiful, is especially vibrant with faery essence.

STRAW

Stories tell of faeries living inside a straw. Straw can be twisted to form an amulet, the simplest shape being an equal-armed cross.

THYME

This Venus-ruled herb will help the wearer to see faeries, so tie a sprig to your button-hole if going to meet them (best not to use a pin).

GORSE

This is said to keep out faeries, because they cannot penetrate the prickles. I find this hard to believe (and so does the gorse faery!).

fOUR-LEAfEO CLOVER

These are very lucky, so if you find such a leaf, treasure it. Seven grains of wheat laid on a clover four-leaf are said to enable one to see faeries. It can also act as a protection against faeries.

BLUEBELLS

In a bluebell wood the entire ground seems to shimmer, as if the sky has come to earth. Such is a place to be possibly 'pixie-led' or led astray by the faeries – something that has happened to not a few folk, who have become hopelessly lost in a locality familiar to them, where well-known landmarks were mysteriously absent. It is not considered advisable to go into a wood to pick these blooms,

COWSLIPS ANO fORGET-ME-NOTS

These can supposedly help you find buried treasure, kept by the faeries.

fOXGLOVES

Definitely the property of the faeries, it is not a good idea to pick these and take them indoors.

WILO THYME, HERB ROBERT ANO RED CAMPION

These plants also belong especially to the faeries, so do not touch them. Robin Goodfellow loves herb Robert and will get upset if you pluck his flower or harm it in any way. Robin Goodfellow has links with pagan figures of the god of nature and the Green Man, debased as a prankster and hobgoblin. This is not to say, of course, that the herb Robert faery isn't especially mischievous and/or jealous!

ST JOHN'S WORT

This herb is said to relieve illnesses sent by the faeries. It can also help in overcoming depression.

Daisies

These pretty little white flowers offer protection against the faeries and a child wearing a daisy chain cannot be kidnapped by them.

Marsh Marigold

If this is placed around the neck of a cow, it will stop the faeries from stealing the milk. Faeries are said to love milk and so it is a good gift to leave for them. However, I dread to think what their reaction is to factory farming!

Faery Trees

Any tree will, I am sure, have its guardian spirit. However, some trees have an especially potent relationship with the faery people.

Oak

Oak, along with ash and hawthorn, is part of the 'Faery Triad'. Where these three trees grow together it is said that one can see faeries. An old saying goes:

> *Turn your cloaks*
> *For fairy folks*
> *Are in old oaks.*

Turning one's coat inside out, and wearing it like this, was believed to be a remedy for being 'pixie-led'.

The oak tree is ancient, powerful and connected to Druid worship which took place in sacred groves. Faeries are reputed to live in oak trees, which have long associations with mythical heroes from King Arthur to Robin Hood and are, of course, a majestic and powerful tree. The mistletoe was especially sacred when found on the oak, symbolizing the moment of incarnation. Another rhyme goes:

> *Ellumm do grieve*
> *Oak he do hate*
> *Willow do walk*
> *If you travels late*

The anger of the Old Gods will fall on anyone who fells the oak tree. The oak has a regal status and deeply resents any injury. An oak coppice, springing from the roots of felled oaks, is held to be a dangerous and sinister place to travel through by night. Oak coppices are haunted by a certain type of malevolent faery called the Oakmen, dwarves with red caps and red noses who tempt travellers with food which is, in reality, disguised fungus. They lurk especially in thrice-cut oak coppices, carpeted with bluebells.

Hawthorn

The twisted shape of the hawthorn speaks of hauntings and eerie passage to Otherworld. The hawthorn is sacred to the Goddess in Her lighter aspect, but it is still considered unlucky to cut the hawthorn before May Eve and, some say, it should not be cut at all.

This tree is perhaps the archetypal faery tree and faeries are believed to inhabit it. Especially dangerous is the lone thorn, standing near a barrow mound, or thorns in groups of three. Such thorns should not be cut or damaged in any way and there is considerable anecdotal and folklore evidence that supports the belief that misfortune will indeed fall on anyone who harms such a tree. It is even considered dangerous to have a snooze under such a tree, for fear of faery retribution. My sense of hawthorn and its faery guardians is not that it is malevolent at all, at least not usually, but that it is magical and venerable and if we do not respect the natural world and learn its laws then we have only ourselves to blame.

Rowan

Rowan is one of the most protective of trees and this is enhanced when it grows near stone circles and similar sites, for it is guardian of the deep Earth energies, which in turn offer it their protection. Many Irish tales tell of dragons protecting rowan trees and the dragon is often a dramatization of the Earth-power itself. Smoke from the rowan can be used to conjure spirits. Generally it is considered the best protection against faery enchantments. Katherine Briggs (see Further Reading) quotes the Scottish rhyme:

Rowan, lamer (i.e. amber) and red threid
Puts witches to their speed

'Red threid' possibly refers to spirit traps, made of red twine. The colour red is supposed to be effective against sprites, which is interesting, as faeries themselves were said to favour red. Some notions may arise from the equating of all spirits and faeries with evil, which was and is common in the dogmatic application of Christianity. Red is the colour of life and, as such, may be considered powerful against anything destructive to life. A rowan staff or rowan berries were all effective. In the Highlands of Scotland rowan trees were planted, where possible, near every house and one of my fondest memories of the Highlands in early autumn is the endless array of beautiful rowan trees, their berries growing like handfuls of rubies. As folklore and custom tend to get all mixed up, and as the gods of the old pagan religions became the devils of the new, we may take it that what works against enchantment is equally full of faery power. This would mean fighting fire with fire. The rowan is a magical tree.

Ash

Ash was used as a substitute for rowan in protecting people from faeries. The ash has an ancient pedigree as the World Tree of Norse legend, from whose branches hung Odin, to gain the secret of the runes. Myth tells how human essence originated from the ash tree. Its pedigree is involved and venerable and it has the faculty of healing our split from the natural world, the split of masculine and feminine and other polarities. Ash unites many elements and its meanings have evolved and adapted as our culture has developed. One can readily imagine that it offers an antidote to the problems caused by our separation from the Faerie realm and its occupants.

Elm and willow

It is said that other elms grieve if one of them is hurt or cut down. Tolkien's Hobbits found that Old Man Willow can cast a dangerous spell, sending the unwary into a magical slumber and swallowing them. Willows are said to up their roots and follow solitary night-time travellers, muttering.

Useful spells

ᗞealing spell

Skin ailments were often thought to be inflicted by the faeries because of some offence against them. Claire Nahmad (see Further Reading) gives this simple spell that enlists the help of the faeries for a cure.

You should find, or best of all make, a little hand-besom of heather. Get up when the Sun rises and be sure that you neither eat a morsel nor say a word. Use your little besom to sweep all the ashes and cinders cleanly into one corner. Now spit upon the swept area and put the forefinger of your right hand into the spittle. Then draw a cross on the affected area of skin with your forefinger, using a touch that is gentle yet firm. Do this on nine successive mornings, to ensure a cure for your skin troubles.

These days an open fire is quite rare, so Claire Nahmad suggests burning a few pine cones in a pot and scattering them on the hearth. With efficient central heating, however, there may be nothing that corresponds at all with a hearth and my only suggestion, in this case, would be to use the cooker, as a focal point of warmth.

In private correspondence Claire has sent me these words:

May I suggest that people using the heather-besom and ash spell create something corresponding to an altar on which to assay its particulars? We find 'heart' in the word 'hearth' as well as 'earth'. The altar should be set up according to however one perceives the Universal Spirit and/or the Goddess. The idea of the fire in the home (it always used to be a central hearth, not the little side fire we have nowadays) was associated with the Sacred Flame ever alight on the altar, the altar being symbolic of the centre or heart of the body of Earth with the eternal flame alight within. The altar would be a good place, but only, I feel, if it was set up as an altar within the spell-worker's consciousness.

This is a helpful passage, reminding us how sacred is everyday life. We may be sure that to our forbears, daily life was a celebration of

the sacred, in the way that Native Americans, especially the Hopi, approach it today. We have largely lost this sense, but we need to reclaim it to contact faeries. All of life is a celebration, everything we do has symbolic meaning. To make your stove into an altar, all that is required is something simple, starting with a change of attitude. Over our stove we have a corn dolly in the shape of a horseshoe, containing the bounty of the Goddess, bound with red ribbon, for the powers of life. Why not place something similar securely over your own stove, setting it up for the spell with candles on either side (I suggest green as a healing colour) and any other pictures or symbols that seem appropriate to you?

OAKLEAF SPELL

Another spell given by Claire Nahmad enables lovers to see the faeries at play. Go together to a lonely place in nature and place inside the shoe of each a single oak leaf. Sit together and talk of your relationship and of your plans and dreams, the closeness you feel. Do this until the stars come out. (I am sure the faeries won't be offended if you make love, but you might miss something!) If you are both patient enough you will see the faeries as they come out to dance and play.

PRACTICE

MEETING THE FAIR FOLK

If you decide that you really want to see faeries this is, I feel, quite a big step. Faeries come in all shapes and sizes and some may be strange and terrible. Even the light-hearted sprite may be mischievous and confusing. However faeries are predominantly positive and contact between the worlds can only be a forward step in our evolution, but this is not a frivolous matter. Certain faeries are reputed to have the power to destroy half the world and such awesome strength may be the property of the beings of the Tuatha de Danaan, the god-like pre-Celtic creatures of myth. Not so long ago people did all they could to protect themselves

from faery contact, partly because all 'spirits' were seen as envoys of Satan in days of religious dogmatism, but also because, in the development of logic and individualism, faeries were of no help. Now we have got to the point where our 'rationality' has outstripped our common sense, so to speak, and we need contact with the subtle realms and the inner world of nature in order to survive as a species and a planet. We are becoming open to the divinity that infuses all of life and of which faeries are a part. However, before we embark on ways to make contact with faeries, let us first look at some modes of protection.

The magic circle is a potent form of protection and in its 'mini' form may be placed around you, by the power of visualization, as if you are inside a protective blue egg. Practise visualizing this, so that you feel strongly that you have a tough 'skin' around you. You may also have a psychic 'cloak', that you don for protection. Brown or green may be preferred colours. Imagine this robe around you when you are psychically exposed in any way. Also select a protective symbol, such as an equal-armed cross, or pentagram (five-point star) and make this symbol individual to you in some way, not by distorting the symbol itself but by superimposing it on, or connecting it to, something that is personal to you. An example might be a gold-armed cross shining amid the blooms of a special plant that was given to you in a spirit of love. Keep the image fairly simple and do not even tell your best friend what it is. Visualize it regularly until you feel sure it is there for you, ready to hold up and protect you when need arises.

In *The Faerie Way* Hugh Mynne makes a suggestion for breaking faery contact, where you visualize your unwelcome faery standing in front of you. Hold an iron knife with its point just above the head of the faery. Now, imagining the head of the faery as in the north, draw a circle about it, from north to east, to south and then to west and back to north again, completely circling the creature. As you do this, see the faery getting smaller and smaller until, as your knife completes the circle, the being is reduced to a speck and disappears. This exercise is a reminder to the faery being that we all travel the cycle of the Goddess and are bound

by natural law. This method is proposed for faery allies that have attached themselves during inward journeys and are later found to be unsuitable. You could adapt it for other circumstances, but cannot, of course, take iron with you when looking for faeries, as they do not like it.

If you erect too many barriers there is, of course, the likelihood that you will neither see nor sense any faery presence. Perhaps the best protection is love and intuition, to which you listen. The 'love' in question is not a woolly New Age benevolence, nor a matter of 'good intentions', but the true radiance of the open heart chakra, infused with love for the world. The positive light of this love serves as its own protection, for where it is flowing outwards, nothing harmful can approach. In respect of intuition, use it. If you feel you are being warned not to visit a certain locality, not to peep, pry or explore, then don't! Traditionally, the faeries have ways of making their preferences felt and, if it is for privacy, do not infringe it on any account. Take note if you feel uneasy or fearful and turn back.

To see faeries you may indeed adopt some of the spells listed above. Perhaps the best approach is to have lots of contact with nature – do not expect to leave your apartment in the city centre, drive out to some beauty spot and have the faeries obligingly materialize in time for you to get back and watch the news before bed-time! Get into the wild and lonely spots of nature as often as you can. Choose somewhere that 'feels right' and/or that has a tradition of faery encounter, such as is often linked to tumuli and other places of antiquity. The west coast of Ireland is supposed to be especially replete with faeries. Expect to go out many times, over a period of weeks, before anything happens, unless you are very psychic. Avoid anything iron, including jewellery, watches, etc. By all means wear thyme, roses or similar and sit quietly in a spirit of peace and meditation. Do not look for the faeries. Just look.

If you do not see faeries, try not to be disappointed. One approach you may adopt is the 'as if' approach. Ask yourself, if there were faeries here, in this place, what form might they take? Imagine

their shapes, their expressions, their actions, their feelings and wishes. The point here is definitely not to superimpose sentimental Victorian images or the products of you own wishful thinking, but to let the place speak through you, causing pictures to arise in you. Sketch them, if you can. Make up poetry or prose to communicate. Leave small offerings. In time, the faeries may reveal themselves and you may find that your 'as if' approach was accurate.

3 NATURE SPIRITS

We call to you, human, from the highest of our realms, and you are there. We call to you from the densest earth, and you are there. We call from other worlds across space, and still you are there. We are inwardly still and attuned, and you share our oneness. If there are worlds we cannot reach, no doubt you are there, too. 'Man, know thyself.'

Words of the Landscape Angel

Those who reach out to us, we lift. When you are in our aura and reach into your being, you are lifted, because we are in a rhythm of harmony. In fact we can aid humans to achieve an inward peace. There should always be large areas where trees reign supreme and undisturbed, where we can give solace to you. Such areas would ultimately do much for the healing of nations.

Words of the Tree Deva
Dorothy Maclean, *To Hear the Angels Sing*

Perhaps the most currently popular and appealing idea of faeries is that they are nature spirits who embody the essences of plants and take care of, on the spiritual plane, the natural world. In the 'alternative' scene it is acceptable to talk to plants, to try to attune to nature spirits when planning a garden or when visiting special sites and even to attempt to contact certain species of spirits, or devas, to obtain a result. While many people are still liable to interpret tales of abduction into Faerieland in a psychological fashion, the idea of spirits in the natural world is taken literally, and

not a few people have experienced encounters, of one sort or another, with these beings. Astrologer Graham Boston describes a meeting with a being he called a *deva* on Glastonbury Tor, one summer's dawn, after spending the night in a tent. The creature was about 1.5 metres (4 feet) in height and its shape was hard to define but was, possibly, egg-shaped. It was green in colour, composed of a network of fine lines and very beautiful. As with such encounters, it felt fairly 'normal' at the time. Graham contemplated the creature for a short while and felt that it was also registering his presence. Then it simply drifted off, down the hill. As it disappeared, the amazing nature of the encounter overwhelmed Graham, together with a feeling of deep peace. He says that he felt very privileged to have had the encounter.

The findhorn Community

The idea of nature spirits rose principally with the Findhorn Community in Scotland, and the story of the wonderful and almost supernatural success in growing plants from barren soil, in inclement conditions, has become a beacon to all those who revere the life within the natural world and seek to co-operate with it. The tale of Findhorn is told by Dorothy Maclean in *To Hear the Angels Sing; an Odyssey of Co-creation with the Devic Kingdom* listed in Further Reading.

While Dorothy's life had led her along a path of increasing spirituality, it was not until she and two friends, Eileen and Peter Caddy, found themselves 'washed up' one winter in Findhorn Bay, about 1.6 kilometres (1 mile) from the Moray Firth in Scotland, that her developing awareness found very practical application. Their dwelling was a caravan, in a trailer park inhabited mostly by Royal Air Force personnel from the nearby air base at Kinloss who were awaiting permanent housing. A set of rather strange coincidences had led to the arrival of the jobless and almost destitute trio, despite the fact they were intelligent and well-qualified people. Their own trailer was in a hollow, at the corner of the park, surrounded by rough plants such as gorse and broom, growing from gravelly soil.

The outlook was flat and bleak and the sky seemed to encase them, with its ever-changing display of clouds. The wind here is almost perpetual, the surrounding landscape lunar and desolate. Legend told how a local laird sold his soul to the devil and as a punishment hundreds of acres of fertile land and many dwellings were covered overnight by silt, brought by mighty gales. While this area of the 'Culbin Desert' was being reclaimed, the land around the caravan was still more like a desert. Nor was there room for them all in the caravan, for Eileen and Peter Caddy had three sons. This meant that Dorothy had to take lodgings in a local hotel. Daily visits to her friends meant hikes over the dunes during a winter so bitter that all the water pipes in the park froze. Despite the hardship and isolation, their interest in changing human consciousness and living harmoniously and creatively with spiritual forces gave them an unabated enthusiasm for life.

Spring came, but when the hoped for jobs did not materialize Peter set about cultivating the land around the trailer, to grow vegetables and augment their food supply. It was hard work, involving removal of the topsoil, so that pebbles could be picked out for about 30 centimetres (1 foot) in depth. Then the original turf was replaced, upside down, and the sand shovelled back in with any compost available. This completed, seeds could be sown for vegetables. It was long and arduous work. Then, during her regular meditation, Dorothy received guidance that she could harmonize with the essence of nature. This developed as more specific guidance concerning actual help with the gardening. This could be accomplished by tuning in to the overlighting spirits of nature and, because this is so unusual in humans, this interest would draw their influences and they would gladly give of their help. Further guidance stated that the higher spirits were the spirits of different physical forms whereas the smaller, individual, nature spirits were under their direction.

Initially Dorothy was reluctant to proceed with this, feeling that she simply could not communicate with these unknown beings. However, she persuaded herself to try to help with the garden in this manner and, because she had always liked peas, she began with an attempt to contact the guiding deva behind this plant. The pea deva told her that the plant kingdom held no grudge against the beings that it fed

and yet man took what he wanted, giving no thanks, which made them 'strangely hostile'. The deva went on to comment that if humans knew where they were going and held to their course, that they would be 'powerhouses' and that the devas would be able to co-operate with them.

After this first contact, communication flowed and specific instructions were given regarding planting and maintaining the vegetables. All instructions were immediately and unquestioningly followed as Dorothy believed that, had this not been the case, help would have been terminated. Dorothy realized that she was in contact with the being that oversaw the entire species, not with the spirit of individual plants. Because her impression was of multi-dimensional creatures of light and joy, she used the Sanskrit word *deva* which means 'shining one' to define them. 'Angel' has also been used to describe such beings. Our terms for the subtle worlds and their inhabitants are liable to be somewhat muddled. However, if one divests 'angel' of its Christmas-card stereotype, it is still debatable whether it is the right word, for there are those who assert that the angels are awesome beings who are not of this world, whereas nature spirits are very much connected to Earth herself.

Dorothy's contact extended to a being that she describes as the Landscape Angel, although this is still very much an Earth spirit. The Landscape Angel was insistent about compost and showed the gardeners how to obtain it. They all became aware that life was a network of spiritual essences, directed consciously by higher beings. The personal energies of each gardener are part of the growth of the garden. Some people put forth life-promoting vibes while others drain their surroundings and may be hostile to plant life. Positive thoughts and feelings do have an effect. A general feeling of thanks and appreciation enhances our connection and is part of the helping process, making us a part of the whole, rather than simply a taker.

The Findhorn garden flourished through continuing co-operation with nature. The County Agricultural Advisor took soil for testing and found that, despite being apparently the same as the soil in the surrounding landscape, it was balanced in respect of necessary nutrients.

Teachings of the devas

The devas imparted much wisdom to Dorothy Maclean and the Caddys and the reality of the fertile garden was a living proof of the truth behind it. Tom Graves in *Needles of Stone* (Gothic Image, 1986) points out that such spectacular results as those of Findhorn have not been easy to duplicate, possibly because Findhorn was a 'pilot scheme', and it is as if the devas were saying, 'This is the kind of thing that we can accomplish, if you will only be aware of us and consciously co-operate with us'. The devas are, no doubt, sickened by the work and attitude of humans. If they were to withdraw their life-force this would have devastating results. The devas taught that what we see as inert clods of earth are teeming with life and light. They are the guiding spirits who oversee the elementals and, while this hierarchical set-up is one way we may perceive the devic kingdom, we still need to bear in mind that our understanding is incomplete. Their task is to build the energy network that underpins the life of the planet, but it is not their job to change patterns. Rather they work within conditions and it is humans who have the power to alter these.

I believe that each person's experience of the non-physical realms is descriptive of that individual to some extent, not because such experiences are merely psychological and subjective, but because we tend to home in on aspects that are expressive of what is inside us. Because the subtle realms are many and varied, there is plenty to choose from and, besides this, there are so many ways of describing an experience, so many differing angles to take. Even in the real world our consciousness shapes our reality and our life formulates itself in accordance with the scripts we have internalized. What we believe, manifests itself although with a time-lag. On the subtle planes, however, manifestation is instant and we encounter our beliefs when we enter them. Thus a person whose concept of Faerie is of strange and tricky beings will find such, while another who is more attuned to guardian spirits and beings of love will find these. Dorothy Maclean states 'different consciousnesses tune into different qualities' and the Landscape Angel demonstrated this to her by showing a side to itself, not previously encountered, that was

'almost cold'. All aspects have their reality and all have something to teach us. Possibly we learn faster from the challenge of the weird and awesome, but devas and nature spirits are, for the most part, pleasant, although they may be stern.

The Universe exists as a wholeness and there is peace and bliss from the realization that one is a part of this. This oneness is a knowledge perpetually lived within the kingdom of nature spirits. Being starts as pattern that evolves to a sound, a vibration, which is taken up by the elementals, who clothe it in form. The devas work in mantras, producing movements, sounds, making a pattern and working up to a certain pitch. Their movements endow their areas with certain qualities of life. We know that all matter is, in essence, vibration. Here we have a picture of the life and vibrancy that is within all, as the early animistic beliefs described. The amazing properties of sound are being explored in connection with the building of the pyramids, where it has been suggested that sound can be used to elevate huge blocks of stone. David Elkington describes, in his forthcoming book *Jesus BC* to be published in 1999 by Curtis Brown, how this was accomplished by him and his colleagues. Sound has long been recognized in magical traditions as having special power. In the *Book of Genesis* we are told, 'In the beginning was the Word, and the Word was God.' Our recognition of existence as a vibrational network is part of the advancement of our consciousness, but also a return to the instinctual wisdom that enabled our forbears to live in closer communion with the Earth and Her guardians.

Dryads, naiads, nereids and oreads

Our forbears were very conscious of the spirits that inhabited certain spots in nature and they were revered as the local goddesses and gods. Wells, streams, groves, hilltops and the seashore all had their inhabiting deity. Druids worshipped in sacred groves, wells were 'dressed' at certain festivals in honour of the Goddess, trees near springs were hung with rags and fragments of raiment in honour of

the local spirit and in hope of blessing. These customs still endure today in many places in Britain and are, in fact, being revived by present-day pagans.

In different parts of the world these spirits of place were conceived of slightly differently. Originally it is quite probable that people revered the spirits of place as part of the omnipresence of the Great Goddess, without intellectually analysing this. Modern pagans may be similar. I don't feel it is necessary to be exact about what deity I sense and worship. It is far more important to get into the feeling and wonder of being part of the natural world. Whether we label this as an aspect of the Great Mother, the goddess Bride, nature spirit or faery may matter poetically but there is no need to be exact about the realm that is beyond our words. These spirits are similar to the people of the Sidhe of Irish legend. The Greeks gave them specific genre names, according to the type of locality and, like many things Greek, their terms have stuck with us.

Dryads were the Greek tree-spirits, *naiads* the water-nymphs, *nereids* the spirits of the shoreline and *oreads* the nymphs of the mountain. These were conceived as beautiful and seductive maidens who existed in the realm between the human and divine. Greek mythology abounds with stories of their interaction with gods and mortals. However, T.C. Lethbridge, the dowser and writer on the paranormal, had a different theory about these creatures.

Traditionally dowsers are concerned with finding underground water, often using a forked hazel rod that twitches when they pass over a buried watercourse. The theory is that the rod does not twitch of itself but due to involuntary movements on the part of the dowser, which are created by his or her unconscious mind in order to communicate. However, this does not explain to me how steel rods, another dowsing tool, will swing of themselves in a moist palm. Dowsers are also concerned with locating energy-fields, ley lines and even with dowsing for allergies, fresh food and other matters of current concern. It was really Lethbridge's work on energy fields that led him into the world of nature spirits.

When he was 18, Lethbridge and his mother were walking through the Great Wood, near Wokingham, Berkshire, when they were both simultaneously overcome with a feeling of extreme depression. A few days later they found out that the body of a suicide victim had been recently discovered at that very spot. Lethbridge later experienced similar, but more acute sensations, at Ladram Bay in Dorset and a more active manifestation on Skellig Michael on the coast of Kerry. On this occasion he felt that something wanted to push him off the cliff, to such an extent that he decided to abandon his journey, but before he could turn round something unseen knocked him to the ground. All these manifestations had occurred near water, or in conditions that were damp or muggy. This led Lethbridge to the theory that water acts in a way similar to a film, recording the emotions of those nearby. This may be especially strong if the emotions are powerful. Such a field would, in a sense, feed on the emotions of fear it engendered and thus grow in power. Lethbridge called such an energy-field a *ghoul*. An example of how a ghoul might develop could be as follows: a person, deeply upset and despairing, hangs themselves from a tree, in the middle of a forest. Trees have a water source close by and held within it by some mechanism as yet unknown to science are the dreadful emotions of the suicide victim and his death experience. Someone else comes along, some while later, perhaps feeling very down. If the conditions are right, for example misty and wet, the energy-field left by the former suicide victim will be especially strong and, to a susceptible individual this could be the last straw, pushing them over into a suicidal frame of mind. Thus the field is newly imprinted with even stronger feelings of doom and despair to influence the next person to come along.

Other similar experiences, recorded by sensitive people in respect of such spots, include the appearance of a greyish light, a feeling of deep evil and being drained of all energy. Something like this was seen by one of my sons and his friends in the local woods, on a damp, grey day. He described it as 'a sort of horrid mist that followed us. It came after us and I saw it, coming out of the trees. Sam said it waits under cars, to feed off people …' I do not doubt that my son really saw something and was uncharacteristically alarmed. The spontaneous embroidery, about hiding under cars and feeding, may

be an instinctive homing in on the ghoulish characteristics of such energy fields by creative teenagers! I gave my son a consecrated holy-stone to wear and advized him about ways to protect himself, among which were the keeping of an open mind and the avoidance of hysteria. Nonetheless, such experiences are not to be trivialized.

Lethbridge felt that the Greek idea of naiads, dryads and nereids had arisen from a perception of these energy-fields that were anthropomorphized by primitive mentality. All of these creatures are associated with water, either above or below ground, and Lethbridge hypothesized that belief in them was merely the result of the interaction between the personal field of the individual and the field of force of the earth at the particular spot. These fields he called 'dryad fields', 'naiad fields' and 'nereid fields'. 'Oread fields', of course, are the exception to the water theory and it may be that Lethbridge included them for the sake of completeness, for they do not seem to feature in case studies.

There is no doubt that places have atmospheres and that any feeling of unease or depression is intensified by wet or misty conditions. These conditions, in certain circumstances, also lend themselves to magical effects, enchantment and romance. We all sense atmospheres in houses or other places and are affected by them. Does this mean that such atmospheres have no independent existence but are merely the sum total of the feelings of people who have inhabited a place or spent time in it? There are those who would say yes, but I think not. While I am sure there is much value in Lethbridge's theory, there would seem to be more to a spirit of place than an amalgam of human emotion. My main reason for this opinion is that certain places and their invisible inhabitants do not feel human at all, but far more strange, terrible, god-like or beneficent than anything originating in the human heart or mind.

PRACTICE

CONTACT WITH THE DEVAS

Contacting devas is not merely for the spaced out or the deeply spiritual. Actual results may be obtainable by anyone who genuinely wishes to make contact. This needs to be in a spirit of love and acceptance but not in a sugary sense that admits to no negativity, but rather in a way that comprises respect and a sensation of joy and openness in the face of the unity of all life.

One of Dorothy Maclean's devic contacts was not a plant spirit but a being called *King Mole* whom she approached in an endeavour to get the moles out of the garden, with good effect. I have certainly had some success with this approach, and so have friends of mine who repeatedly 'persuaded' invasive ants to move elsewhere. This is far better than trying to exterminate creatures, for a variety of reasons, not least practical ones. For instance, at Findhorn wasps were expelled, which resulted in a plague of caterpillars, on whom the wasps feed. By contacting the species deva, troublesome creatures can be persuaded to move some way away. A bargain must always be made – for instance if you wish to be rid of ants you may ask the ant deva to keep them out of the house on the understanding that you will never intentionally kill an ant.

If you are used to meditating, shamanic journeying or creative visualization, it will probably come naturally to you to contact such beings. If not, here are some guidelines. Firstly, choose a time and a place where you can be peaceful and undisturbed for perhaps half an hour. If you need something to enhance your mood, you may like to burn a joss-stick and light a candle, but this is not absolutely necessary. Close your eyes and relax deeply. Tell yourself that you wish to contact the deva of a particular species and see what images form in your mind. Please remember that this can be surprisingly scary, especially if the species in question is one of which you are especially afraid, as many people are of spiders, snakes, rats and such like. The deva is likely to appear to you as a huge member of the species, probably much

larger than you. It will not harm you, but it may be quite hostile, especially if you have been killing off its creatures.

Now try to set up some communication with the deva. You may find that you spontaneously know what the being is communicating and that it all happens very quickly, or you may have to wait patiently for an answer. Frame your request and state your bargain clearly. You may feel that another bargain is asked by the deva – for instance non-interference may not suffice and the deva may require some specific care from you for the species in return for leaving you alone. You may hear this or know it or you may see it in writing, if you are very visual. Non-physical beings do not always spell very well! If you do not understand what is being communicated, take notes, for you may work this out at a later time. If there is no response at all from the deva, still make your bargain clear and say that you will abide by it. Terminate contact respectfully and come back to everyday awareness. If your experience has been vivid this may be unsettling, especially if you are not used to such work. You may have discovered a talent within yourself. Take care of yourself by consciously bringing yourself back, down to earth. Pat yourself from head to toe, touch the ground, have something to eat and drink.

Now you must keep the bargain you have made to the letter. I do not think the bargain will be void if you accidentally break it and apologize, but too much carelessness may certainly destroy the bond and the deva may not wish to co-operate further. Sometimes it takes a while for the species to respond and I suppose that while devas operate in a world outside our space and time the relevant species is very much within our time-frame. It is worthwhile noting that such contact, even though it is getting rid of the creature in question, slowly develops into a bond with it and the little acts of service that you perform as your side of the bargain make you feel affection even for pests and creepy-crawlies!

If you do the exercise as I have suggested but feel nothing happens and that you have no contact with any deva, still state your bargain clearly and, if you wish, audibly. You may not be

conscious of achieving contact, but nonetheless you may have made it. Keep to your bargain and see what happens. There is no harm in making repeated attempts to contact devas. If there is no visible result it may be because, for some reason, the species in question cannot survive locally by moving elsewhere. With practice you may achieve more detailed contacts which will help you to understand and live in harmony.

PLANT HEALING

At our shamanic group, the Moon Lodge, we were celebrating the feast of Samhain, or Hallowe'en, marking the change in the seasonal tide, the moving within and underground of the life-force and the coming time of darkness. Samhain is a major pagan festival worshipping the cycles of nature and, while it is a time to confront and honour the forces of death, decay and transmutation, it is also a time to honour the life-force itself and to affirm this, in the shadows of the darkening year. In this spirit one of our company brought along a special plant she had, in which the totality of the cycle of life seemed to be embodied in several ways, for there were dead bits, flourishing bits and the twisting tendrils and glimpses of serpentine root spoke of passage into another world. We passed the plant around, describing it as creatively as we could, giving it our total attention, stating our impressions of it, imaginatively and physically and generally sending love and blessing towards it.

We passed the plant around our circle several times and it was amazing how many things we all found to say. As we began to exhaust physical description, our impression of the essence of the plant came through more strongly and we gained a feel for its personality or for the deva or nature spirit that was linked to it. From being a humble entity, stuck in a pot, the plant swelled until it was almost an Otherworld portal. We were conscious that the plant itself was becoming more vibrant and its deva filled with joy, not merely at the attention given to the specific little plant but at the contact that humans were taking the time and trouble to make with the plant kingdom and the subtle realms.

From this little exercise we all felt enriched. If you have a plant that is ailing, for no reason that you can identify, it is certainly worth trying this approach. You could do it with friends, or alone. Rather than merely pouring love into it (which may be conducive to benevolent self-righteousness) try to be receptive to the plant, as we were, in essence, as we described it. Touch the plant with your left hand (if you are right-handed) and you may get a strong impression of what the needs of the plant may be. You might also do a journey to the deva of the plant, as suggested above, to find out more. Pour as much positive feeling and creative attention into the plant as you can and see if this has a healing effect. It is probable that the plant will indeed benefit, for science has shown some evidence that plants absorb impressions and respond to the attentions of their carers. It will certainly enhance your appreciation of the interconnectedness of life and its wonder.

4

SYMBOLIC
INTERPRETATION
OF FAERY TALES

*The biggest problem of making internal maps of reality is not that
we have to start from scratch, but that if our maps are to be
accurate we have continually to revise them.*

M. Scott Peck, *The Road Less Travelled*

One modern approach to faery tales, which has found acceptance
with many psychotherapists, is to regard them as symbolic of
what is going on inside the human mind. Dreams can be interpreted
as indicating processes that are going on within the subconscious
mind of the individual and faery stories are rather like a dream of
the collective mind, stories that are compelling and pervasive
because they have symbolic meaning for all people. Such stories are
full of archetypal contents, which means that they include powerful,
universal templates that are common to the unconscious of
humanity. This type of approach effectively visualizes us as
connected as profoundly as islands are connected to the same mass
of land beneath the sea. Certain symbols mean the same to us,
whether we are Native American, Chinese, Irish, English, Aborigine
or whatever. For instance, the faery tale *Cinderella* exists in many
versions and was already old when it was first written down in
China in the ninth century CE. This approach was put forward by
C.G. Jung, erstwhile disciple of Freud and pioneer of analytical
psychology. Jung upheld, however, that the contents of the psyche
were objective and he had psychic experiences himself. However, it
may be fruitful to regard faery stories from a symbolic angle, to see
what we may learn.

PERSONAL TALES

Janet Bord (see Further Reading) lists several instances where faeries have been a convenient psychological device for people under stress. This is not to regard the tale as being one that is consciously fabricated, but rather that the experience arises spontaneously in someone who is especially needy. One woman who had recently lost a relative began to see a leprechaun called Murgatroyd, who claimed to be descended from the Tuatha de Danaan, although as he was only 60 centimetres (2 feet) tall, and these beings are majestic and mighty, this seems unlikely. Murgatroyd always appeared dressed in green and tan and at times when the lady was either very upset or very joyful. Murgatroyd was passed on to this woman as a sort of legacy from the deceased relative. A psychotherapist interpreted Murgatroyd as being a psychological defence against manic depression. As he was handed down to the woman he also represented a form of belonging, linking her to the family tree. He was a guardian spirit of the family and protection for the woman's individuality. We may assume from this that the leprechaun had no objective reality of any sort and was merely something the patient dreamed up, to protect her from going crazy.

Another account tells of a child who had her own special elf. Being the eldest child, she often found her wish for attention had to come behind the needs of her younger siblings, especially at bed-time. One night a little man with black, shiny eyes appeared on the headboard of her bed. He wore bright clothes, a crooked hat and on his feet were shoes with square, shining buckles. Far from being frightening, he was delightful, and told her lots of entertaining stories, until she fell asleep. When she reached out to him he evaded her touch and told her not to try to touch him. On the final night he came to her saying that another child now needed him more than she did and that this was the last time she would ever see him. He vanished and she never saw him again.

Both of these stories could well relate to mental devices, projected by the minds of those who saw them. However, we may be entering muddy waters here. The interpretation of such phenomena is a

fertile area where we may discover many things about the workings of the mind. However, we have a lot to learn about mental illness. While an open mind and a questioning attitude is essential, it may be that what is thought of as illness may be more of a talent than a disorder and one that would have been deeply venerated in the world of the Neolithic shaman.

Beauty and the Beast

The story of Beauty and the Beast is a favourite for analysis. It is a simple, magical tale of enchantment but it has meanings which are deeply symbolic and applicable to the inner lives of all, to a greater or lesser extent. This is the story.

Beauty is a young girl, the youngest of four daughters, and she is her father's favourite because she is unselfish and good. While the other girls ask for costly presents of gold, jewels and fine clothes, Beauty asks only for the gift of a white rose. Beauty is sincere and full of love and has no idea that she could be endangering her father's life. Beauty's father knows that the most lovely rose of all grows in an enchanted garden. As he stealthily enters the garden all seems peaceful, the bees hum and the sun shines. On the rose bushes grow the finest blooms ever seen and Beauty's father selects the most radiant, perfect flower, to pick for his favourite daughter.

As he plucks the rose and turns to make his way out of the garden, a fearsome, hideous Beast strides out in front of him. Terrified, the father tries to run, but he cannot escape. The dreadful creature holds him fast in its claws and demands to know why he has stolen the most splendid rose from the magical garden of which he, the Beast, is king.

'I – I am sorry,' stutters the father, 'I had no idea. I just wanted the best rose for my daughter. I meant no harm.'

'You meant no good, either,' rejoins the Beast. 'You came into my garden to steal what is mine, without asking, by deceit. You thought only of your own concerns and the wishes of your daughter. For that you shall die.'

'Please,' begs the father, 'please let me at least go to my daughter and tell her what has happened. If I am to die, let me give her the rose for which I am to lay down my life.'

For a moment the terrible Beast pauses. Then he loosens his grip on the man. 'Very well,' he replies. 'You shall have your wish. Go to your daughter with the rose and your story, but give me your word that, in three months, you will return, for your punishment.'

With a heavy heart the father agrees. He leaves the enchanted garden, returns to his humble home and, with sorrow in his eyes, presents Beauty with the glorious flower. Beauty sees that he is troubled. 'What is the matter, father?' she asks. When he will not tell her she begs and pleads, until the awful truth is revealed. On hearing of his bargain, Beauty bursts into tears.

'You shall not go back,' she cries. 'It was for me you stole the rose so I shall return in your stead and take the punishment.'

At the end of the three months Beauty makes ready to go to the castle of the Beast, with great fear in her heart, but also with determination. As she comes to the gates of the enchanted garden it seems to her that a mist descends over the beauty of the flowers that grow there and she feels a chill of dread. However, holding good to her resolve, she proceeds up the path towards the castle door but, before she gets to it, the Beast springs out in front of her. He is even uglier and more ghastly than her father had described, but she does not run. Instead she follows the beckoning Beast, as he leads her through the heavy castle door and its shadowy hall, into the most beautiful room imaginable.

Day after day, by the window she waits for her fate, gazing out at the panorama of hill and dale that spreads before her by daylight and at the glory of the Moon and stars at night. She is brought delicious food, lovely clothes of silk and satin in all the colours of the rainbow and, gradually, she comes to enjoy herself and to realize that the Beast has no intention of killing her. She has no worries at all, but she fears the repeated visits of the Beast, who wishes her to marry him. Despite the fact that she is growing close to the Beast, appreciating his gentleness and care, she cannot ignore the repulsiveness and fearsomeness of his appearance.

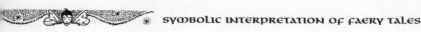

The Beast has a magic mirror in which Beauty can observe the events of the world outside the enchanted castle and, one day, she sees her father lying sick unto death. She begs the Beast to let her go to him and he agrees on condition that she will come back in a week. The Beast tells her that he will die without her. When she returns home her beauty and radiance bring joy and recovery to her father but also arouse jealousy in her three sisters. The sisters plot and scheme to keep her there, believing that this will cause disaster. Sure enough, Beauty outstays the promised week, enjoying being at home with her family. However, in her dreams she sees that the Beast is dying of misery and she knows that she must go back.

When she returns to the castle, she finds the Beast lying upon his bed, in great pain and weakness, close to death. Weeping, she does her best to revive him, quite forgetting that he is ugly. He says that he can now die happy, knowing that she is there, for he was unable to live without her. A great shadow falls over the heart of Beauty and she realizes that she cannot live without the Beast for, despite his fearsomeness, she has fallen in love with his gentleness and his inner radiance. She tells him that, if only he will not die, she will marry him.

At this music and light fill the air and an unearthly glow shines about the Beast. It shimmers and dances around his poor, hideous, form until the Beast disappears to be replaced by a handsome prince, who rises, tall, strong and joyful, from the bed.

'Ah, Beauty,' exclaims the prince, 'you have broken the spell. Long ago an old woman came to my castle asking for shelter and I refused her, repelled by her ugliness. She turned into a faery enchantress and told me that appearances are often deceptive and that I was a fool to judge by them alone. Then, as a punishment, she turned me into a vile Beast and decreed that I should stay that way until a beautiful girl should love me solely for my goodness. This you have done and the spell is broken.'

Beauty and her Prince embraced. There was great celebration and merriment throughout the land and they lived happily ever after.

MEANINGS OF THE STORY

As with so many myths, there are lots of possible meanings and discerning them is rather like peeling away the layers of an onion. One of the principal interpretations of the story involves the concept of the Shadow.

The Shadow is a part of each personality. It consists of all that we fear and repress about ourselves, all that we are unwilling to acknowledge, all that we regard or have been taught to regard as reprehensible. It is hard to convey quite the ambience of this without recourse to fairy story and imagery, because fear of the Shadow has a horror about it that is usually quite unjustified by what the Shadow actually is. For instance, a simple human emotion such as jealousy could become part of the Shadow if, for reasons connected with childhood conditioning, an individual came to regard their own jealousy as so unacceptable and dangerous that it could not possibly be acknowledged. A possible scenario might be the birth of a younger sibling, towards whom the infant felt extreme jealousy and murderous intent, as older siblings often, understandably, do.

Sibling rivalry is enshrined in the story of Cain and Abel. However, it is not usual for older children to try to kill the little one. Yet if an accident should befall the little one, such as a fall, that coincided with a bout of violent hatred on the part of the older child, this child could become convinced that they were responsible for the harm or demise of the smaller one. For a child, this might be too dreadful to contemplate, especially if the prevailing climate among the adults was highly disturbed, as well it might be. So the whole package of jealousy, hatred and rage is rigorously repressed and forced into the subconscious.

All well and good, we might say, best to push things like jealousy and hatred well out of the way, thank you! However, it is not that simple, because unacceptable feelings do not go away when they are repressed but, like a mad relative locked up in a cellar, they manage to cause considerable disturbance and unease to the family upstairs. Such emotions are understandable and natural. After all, to a small child, withdrawal of parental care is a real threat to survival

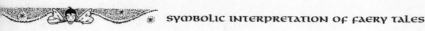

and a new arrival in the family may seem to signal this threat. While we choose not to express certain feelings, that is different to repressing them. Jealousy becomes part of the Shadow, something quite impossible to acknowledge. The Shadow is often projected which means that the person concerned sees it in people outside, but never in themselves, and recoils from it in righteous horror. This person probably has a talent for unconsciously arousing jealousy in others and, while this plays havoc with relationships, it is yet considerably better than acknowledging the Shadow.

However, until the Shadow is acknowledged, there is no way that this person can form reasonable relationships. Because so much mental and emotional energy is going into keeping the Shadow at bay lots of creativity, energy and resources become inaccessible. It is impossible to repress selectively and what tends to happen is that the repressive mechanism operates rather like a vacuum cleaner, sucking into the Unconscious all sorts of desirable qualities as well. The Shadow is also called The Dweller on the Threshold. Until the Shadow is dealt with it is debatable whether we can work effectively upon ourselves and get at other unconscious contents. We all have a Shadow and discovering it may be a repulsive process, of fear and self-loathing. Most uncomfortably, what we most hate in other people often turns out to be our own Shadow. However, in most cases, the Shadow isn't that dreadful after all. Good qualities, that for some reason we think we cannot possess, may also be part of the Shadow. Once confronted and valued, the Shadow may turn into something empowering and rich, our gateway to the kingdom of our own potential. I am sure that, by now, you have guessed that the Beast is none other than the Shadow.

fURThER mEANINGS

In the happy ever after scenario, we also have the marriage of the two sides of the personality, the conscious feminine and the unconscious masculine, or the reverse if the individual is male. Union with our unconscious contra-sexual counterpart also means

balance within the personality. The image of the beautiful princess and the handsome prince, and the land in joy and celebration at their wedding, is a symbol that is compelling and magnetic. This is more than romantic wishful thinking; it is a real impulse towards balance and the union of opposites. Polarization has brought much harm to our world, resulting in wars, persecution and the despoiling of the Earth. Matter and spirit have been regarded as split, separate and as opposites to each other, with matter labelled as evil and inferior. Where we discern that all is interconnected and joined, then we realize how much we are a part of the web of life. When we see the sacredness of the material world as the abode of the Goddess, pollution and similar ills are no longer an issue.

Faeries, in all their forms, show us the life within the Earth and throughout the Cosmos and how we all depend upon each other. They can bring planetary awareness. The marriage of the prince and princess is also, as in times of yore, the marriage of the king with the sacred land, the Goddess, from whom he drew his power and authority. Faeries can re-introduce us to the power of the Earth, from whom we draw our life and connect us to what Bob Stewart (see Further Reading) calls 'the inner realm of ever-becoming, of transformation, of boundless potential'.

And we can all live happily every after!

PRACTICE

It may be that faery stories are a collection of powerful symbols, thrown up by our unconscious minds, in order to communicate with us. Or it may be that the Faerie realm is objectively real, albeit in another order of existence and that we can learn much about ourselves and our world through interaction. Either way, much teaching is symbolic.

If you are interested in symbols, you may like to contemplate the symbols in the story more extensively. Often it is better to consider the elements in the story in freeze-frames, separating them from the narrative. Some elements to consider might be:

- **Three sisters**. Why three? Clues: Triple Goddess, creative nature of number symbolism of '3'. Three daughters, plus father, make 4 and we saw in our chapter on Magic how 4 is the basis for the magic circle. It is also the basis for Jung's description of the human psyche as having four functions of consciousness.

- **Magic mirror**. Clues: The only way we are able to see ourselves is in a mirror, otherwise we are always gazing outwards. We can also see behind us. The mirror is sometimes the gateway to another dimension in stories (e.g. Alice Through the Looking-Glass). Vampires have no reflection.

- **The white rose**. Flowers have many meanings, and some of those attached to the rose have been given. Which others can you think of?

- **The enchantress**. Behind the story is an old crone who tests the prince. When he fails she turns into a lovely, but terrible, enchantress. Through her cruel punishment, the prince finds a depth of love he could never have encountered without being turned into a Beast. For as a handsome prince, with a kingdom of his own, any maiden would have been eager to become his wife but he would never have known whether he was loved for himself. What else can you make of the identity of the enchantress?

To explore these matters you may like to start with *Man and His Symbols*, edited by C.G. Jung, (Picador, 1978) and Tom Chetwynd's *Dictionary of Symbols* (Paladin, 1982). However, as symbols are personal things it is better to arrive at your own interpretation and reaction rather than to instruct yourself intellectually. Play with the ideas and see what arises for you.

5

STORIES FROM FAERY TRADITIONS

How beautiful they are,
The lordly ones,
Who dwell in the hills,
In the hollow hills

From 'The Faery Song' taken from *The Immortal Hour* by Fiona Macleod, as given by R.J. Stewart in *The Living World of Faery*

IRELAND

The Irish take a mythological approach to their heritage, for in the mists of the past there is an interweaving between the dimensions. Stories are told of successive invasions by divine or partly divine creatures, strange and fantastical, who drove out their predecessors. These may be taken as a symbolic account of the evolution of modern consciousness, or as real activities of types of the Fair Folk. In a strange way I believe it may be both.

The first mythical race was the Cessair, followed by the Partholon, the Nemed, the Fir Bolg and the Tuatha de Danaan. All of these, except the Fir Bolg, had trouble with a race of primitive and terrifying creatures called the Fomhoire, conquered finally by the Tuatha de Danaan at the battle of Magh Tuiredh (Moy Tura). With the arrival of the Sons of Miled the Tuatha de Danaan are driven away. Amergin, the bard of the Milesians, proclaims the unity of human and Cosmos in the Song of Amergin, as they land on Irish shore: 'I am a stag: of

seven tines … I am a hill: where poets walk.' The Tuatha de Danaan become the People of the Sidhe, shining beings who interact with humans and dwell deep within the hollow hills, from which they come and go mysteriously, at will. Here is one such faery story of human's brush with Faerie.

The tale of Midhir and Etain

Midhir was a faery lord, of the hill of Bri Leith and the beautiful Etain was his second wife, who incurred the bitter enmity of his first wife, the sorceress Fuamnach. Fuamnach turned Etain into a fly and blew her, with a bitter wind, into the land of Ireland and of mortality. For seven years she was buffeted about, in a state of extreme misery, until she was blown into the hall of Inver Cechmaine, owned by Etar. Into the cup of Etar's wife fell Etain and she was swallowed with her wine, to be born as her daughter, in due course. Meanwhile the evil Fuamnach was beheaded.

The reborn Etain was duly called by her faery name, although she had no recollection of her real origins. She became the most beautiful woman across the length and breadth of Ireland. Midhir appeared to her, but she did not recognize her former husband, although the burning eyes of the faery lord haunted her memory. She married Eochaid, but Midhir always watched her, knowing her whereabouts. After the marriage Eochaid's younger brother Ailell fell deeply in love with Etain so that he became ill and, while Eochaid was away, Etain agreed to meet him for it seemed the only way to restore him to health. However, on the night of the tryst, Ailell fell into a deep sleep. Etain was approached by a man, in great pain, but when he was close to her she perceived that this was not Ailell, after all. She and the stranger looked in silence at each other until he moved on. Etain returned to the castle to find Ailell newly risen and very angry with himself. Again they agreed to meet, and again the same thing happened. On the third occasion Etain spoke to the stranger.

'I came here to meet another,' she said, 'not for wantonness, but to heal sickness.'

'Come back with me, Etain,' the stranger replied, 'for I am your lover and your lord from long, long ago. I am Midhir of Bri Leith. You were blown from Tir Na Nog through sorcery, and I have long sought you.'

But Etain would not go with him. When she returned to Ailell she found that he was cured of the spell placed upon him and they both rejoiced because they had not betrayed Eochaid. However, Midhir did not give up. Once again he appeared to Etain, asking her if she would go with him, were Eochaid to release her. Believing that Eochaid would never do this, Etain agreed. Midhir left, but soon after a stranger called upon Eochaid and challenged him to a game of chess. The stakes they played for were high and, by tradition, were named by the winner after the game was over. Eochaid won two games. The first time he asked for a great tribute of horses, the second time for immense tasks that taxed the abilities of Midhir's faery hosts. However, the third game was won by Midhir, who duly asked for Eochaid's wife. When Eochaid refused Midhir settled for the right to put his arms around her and kiss her and a time for this was set.

Eochaid no doubt realized that he was dealing with a faery and he secured his castle and drew about him his finest fighting men in case Midhir should try to spirit away his wife. Midhir arrived on the appointed day, drew his sword with his left hand, put his right arm around Etain and kissed her. The two rose through the roof and were spotted flying away, over Tara, in the form of two white swans linked by a golden chain.

Eochaid could not rest without his wife and tracked the couple down to Bri Leith, declaring war on the hosts of Faerie, digging relentlessly into the emerald slopes of the faery hill. Despite the frantic digging, however hard his men worked and however deep they went, the holes were always filled the next morning and they had to start all over again. At length, because of the trouble caused, Midhir struck a bargain with Eochaid and returned Etain to him. But a doom is laid upon Eochaid and all his descendants and Midhir appears to him and convinces him that he has not lain with his wife, but his daughter, born in Faerie where time passes differently. The saga of Midhir and Etain continues, as successive reincarnations of Etain meet, mate with and are separated from Midhir by the gulf between this world and Otherworld. Yet the worlds eternally interweave.

The Mabinogion

The Mabinogion is a collection of traditional Welsh stories, drawn from the White Book of Rhydderch and the Red Book of Hergest. These were written in the fourteenth century but their content is very much older and is hailed as some of the finest examples of Celtic creativity. Several of the stories were later embellished as part of the Arthurian saga. The story I have chosen is very ancient, concerning the mythology of a god-like figure, one of the race of giants, called Bran (or Bendigeidfran) and his destiny is intertwined with that of the British Isles. It comes from the section of the Mabinogion called *Branwen, Daughter of Llyr* and it illustrates, among other things, the importance the Celts gave to the head, as the seat of eloquence and wisdom. It is also a story about a special kind of faery, a giant, with magical powers.

The tale of Bran the Blessed

Bran was given the crown of London and so great was his size that no dwelling was large enough to accommodate him. He was a genial representative of the race of giants, who possessed treasures that brought magical gifts to the land of Britain. One of these was a Cauldron of Healing that came from Ireland and had the property of returning the dead to life. Bran had a sister Branwen, a brother Manawyddan and two half-brothers called Nissyen and Evnissyen. The former was a peacemaker but the latter loved to create strife.

Branwen was married to Matholwch, King of Ireland, but during their wedding feast Evnissyen, who had not been consulted about the match, set upon the Irishmen's horses and mutilated them in a frenzy of rage. This was a terrible injury and Matholwych and his followers withdrew to the Irish fleet and were only pacified by the offer of the Cauldron of Healing as recompense. The royal couple accordingly sailed for home, but as time went by the Irish sense of outrage only grew. After the birth of their son, Gwern, Matholwych allowed himself to be persuaded to reject Branwen. Every indignity imaginable was heaped upon the unfortunate princess and no visitor

from Britain was ever allowed to return, in case they told the tale to Bran. But Branwen trained a starling to fly with a message under its wing and, at length, it brought news to Bran of his sister's plight.

Then Bran fell into a mighty rage. Gathering together his hosts, he led his fleet to sea, wading through the water, for so great was his size he needed no ship to carry him. Soon a message came to Matholwych that something awesome was approaching across the sea. This was described as a forest in motion with a tall headland rising behind, at the peak of which was a ridge of rock, between two lakes. Having a 'bad feeling' about this, Matholwych asked his estranged wife for an explanation and she immediately told him.

'The forest is a mighty fleet, gathered against you by my brothers. The headland is my giant of a brother, Bran. The rocky ridge is his nose and the lakes are his great eyes, in a passion of anger.'

In a panic the Irish retreated across the river Linon, demolishing the bridge behind them. But Bran stretched himself over the torrent and his armies crossed safely to the other side. Matholwych knew he had met his match and so delivered himself to atone for the Irish wrongdoings, abdicating in favour of his little son and offering to build a huge house to shelter Bran, while a peace agreement was signed. Bran acquiesced, but Evnissyen discovered that warriors were hidden inside leather bags, hanging from the pillars of the great house, and he surreptitiously went and crushed the skull of each of them.

Peace was signed and the British and Irish were making merry, as little Gwern, the new king, went from kinsman to kinsman, smiling happily. When he came up to Evnissyen his uncle grabbed him by the heels and flung him bodily into the centre of the great fire. At this outrage every man present snatched up his arms and the battle raged long and bloody. The Irish dead were put into the Cauldron and restored, but none of the Welsh were saved. Remorse overtook Evnissyen and not before time, one might say! He threw himself down among his enemies and though he was, at length, thrown into the Cauldron he burst it and his own heart at the same time.

The tide now turned in favour of the Britons, but it was too late and too little. Bran was mortally wounded by a poisoned arrow in the foot.

Knowing that he was dying he bade his companions cut off his head and bury it beneath the White Tower in London. In Ireland all that was left were five pregnant women and these founded the Five Kingdoms. Of the Welsh only eight survived, including Branwen, and when she returned home her poor heart burst with grief to think of the destruction of the two nations, through her unwilling agency.

As for Bran, his head was duly carried to London and buried in the White Mount, where some say it rests to this day. As long as the head of Bran remains as guardian, no threat can ever menace the Island of Britain.

Scotland

As a Celtic country, Scotland abounds with faery lore. Here I have chosen three stories, two concerning faery abductions and the third a traditional tale about sea creatures called *Selkies*.

Faery Wives

A Lothian farmer's wife had been taken away by the faeries. However, her great love drew her back to her children and during the first year of her absence she was often seen among them, combing their hair. Her husband came up to her and demanded to know what had happened. She explained that the faeries had taken her, but there was a way to get her back. It is well known that at Hallowe'en the boundaries between this world and Otherworld dissolve. The old name for Hallowe'en is Samhain, meaning Summer's End and this is the Celtic New Year as well as the time at which ancestors are honoured. On this magical night the farmer had to lie in wait for a procession of faeries, to rescue his wife as she passed by with them. However, when he saw the ghostly procession and heard the unearthly sounds his heart failed him and, though he dearly loved his wife, he remained rooted to the spot. After they had passed him by, there was the sound of wild laughter and, rising above the rest, he heard the voice of his wife wailing that now he had lost her forever.

The Laird of Balmachie, on the other hand, appears to have been made of sterner stuff. The Laird set off for Dundee one day, leaving his sick wife at home in bed. On his return, something prompted him to leave the high road and, riding among the knolls, he came upon a troop of faeries, bearing a litter. He drew his sword and laid it upon the litter, crying in ringing tones, 'In the name of God, release your captive.'

At this, the faeries dropped their burden and vanished. Dismounting from his horse the Laird found that it was his own wife on the litter. He wrapped her in his coat and rode safely home with her, but he was too wise to assume that all was well. Leaving his wife in the care of an attendant, he strode to the sick-room, where it seemed his wife still lay, ill with a fever. She berated him for leaving her and complained how poorly she felt. The Laird feigned great sympathy and had his servants build a roaring fire. Then he lifted his wife as if to put her on a chair, close to the blaze, but instead he threw her into the flames. She shot straight through the roof. Then he went to his true wife, who was beginning to recover. She told him how a throng of elves had come in through her window and lifted her up, from when she remembered nothing until her husband had rescued her. This tale has a happy ending, except that the hole in the roof made by the escaping faery reappeared every year, in company with a tempest that injured nothing else. The hole had to be constantly repaired. (Both of these stories are adapted from Katherine Briggs, see Further Reading.)

The Selkie

The Selkies are magical creatures of Orkney and Shetland. Their natural form is humanoid, but they put on sealskins in order to move through the water. Hauntingly beautiful, these creatures were known to mate with humans and to awaken in them a yearning for Otherworld. Like other faeries many believed them to be angels, fallen from Heaven. The following story is also found in *Reach Your Potential Pisces,* (Hodder & Stoughton, 1998) and derives, I believe, from traditional Scottish sources.

Once upon a time, on the roof of the world, a solitary hunter stopped to rest near the shore. He could not believe what he saw, for on the moonlit beach danced a group of slender, naked women. The hunter had heard tales of how seals, with their soulful eyes, were once human. There on the white sands lay several skins, one for each of the glistening dancers. Filled with yearning, the hunter crept from his hiding place and snatched up one of the skins, buttoning it inside his coat. Then he waited.

The dance was over and with silvery laughter the women retrieved their skins – all except one, the most beautiful of all. When all her companions had slipped beneath the waves the hunter stepped out into the open.

'I have your skin,' he said. 'Come with me. Be my wife and after seven years I will give you back your skin and you may do as you wish.'

What could the seal-maiden do? She agreed and went with the hunter to his dwelling, where they lived together happily enough. A son was born to them, but yet there was sorrow in the great eyes of the seal woman and her lovely skin cracked and became opaque. At the end of the seven years she begged her husband for her sealskin, but he became angry and would not return it. The seal woman pined and sorrowed, but her son who loved her, overheard them talking. He followed his father to where he had hidden the skin, unearthed it and gave it back to his mother.

Seizing the skin with delight she slipped into it and ran for the shore. But the boy ran after her crying, 'Mother, don't leave me – take me with you.' She hesitated, breathed her magic breath into his mouth and took him with her, beneath the waves.

In the underwater world, too wondrous to describe, the boy learnt many things. However, he knew he could not stay forever, for his destiny lay in the upper world, with his father. So after a while his mother brought him back to the shore. Kissing him, she took sorrowful leave.

His bereft father rejoiced to see him and the boy adapted to life on land once more. But every time he looked out on the moonlit tide he could feel his mother, close by. At length he became a famous musician and his greatest joy was to sit upon the shore, playing his pipes, watching the seal people dancing, far out on the waves.

PRACTICE

As we have observed elsewhere, the characteristics of faeries vary, often in harmony with the landscape. The above is a small, and not necessarily representative, selection of traditional tales. Some say that Irish faeries are gentler and more romantic linked with the beauty of the western coast, while Scottish faeries, from the harsh, dramatic Highlands, are more frightening. While faeries are not, of course, a solely Celtic phenomenon, the Celtic lands would appear to be the richest in most types of faery lore. Wales, Scotland, Brittany, Cornwall and the Isle of Man, as well as Ireland, have a plentiful store of faery stories. If you wish to probe deeply into faery tales, why not start with a country and a landscape that you find especially appealing and use this as a starting point for your attunement to the world of Faerie? The countryside will enhance your appreciation of the tales, as the stories themselves make the hills and valleys come to life.

A FAERY GLOSSARY

There is a wealth of tradition regarding faeries and their practices. Here is a selection of definitions in faery lore.

CAPTIVES IN FAERIE

Faeries were said to covet the young, beautiful or talented and might steal them away to live with them. Young men or women might be lured away by faery princesses or princes who fell in love with them. The musically gifted were especially coveted by the faeries. Faeries would take people to work for them, or fight for them, for faery factions seem to be eternally battling. Some believed that there was also a nastier reason for the taking of humans, for these could be given in lieu of faeries as tribute, due every seven years, to the Devil. This view, however, arises from a dualistic perception that is unlikely to have been part of the most ancient material. New mothers were in especial danger of abduction, in order to suckle faery babies, and the most perilous time was in the first days after giving birth. Giving birth is a cross-over point and one that is psychologically fraught. It is easy to lose something, in identification with the baby and the adoption of the new role as mother. Post-natal depression is common and post-natal psychosis not unusual. This serves as a psychological interpretation for the stories. However, maybe after giving birth one is simply closer to Faerieland ....

Co-walker

This is a faery double, similar to a *doppelganger* looking in every way like its human equivalent. *Doppelgangers* have been equated with the journeying forth of the astral body of the subject, in a form visible to others, perhaps by a mechanism similar to the use of ectoplasm by a materialization medium. Traditionally, however, the co-walker is none other than a faery. In times of yore, contact with faeries was generally feared and avoided, but now it may be sought as a means of healing the wounded Earth and our own divided souls. Hugh Mynne, in *The Faerie Way*, gives instructions for meeting and uniting with the co-walker, along with other faery allies.

Faery Lover

There are many accounts of matings between mortals and immortals, usually with tragic consequences. Often heroes are endowed with faery women of ethereal beauty as wives, or faery kings steal human women of exceptional beauty, to be their mistress. One dangerous form of faery is the Manx *lhiannan-shee*, an irresistibly beautiful spirit who can steal the body and the soul of the man who is seduced by her. The Irish version, the *leanan-sidhe*, is regarded more as a muse and inspiractrice, who the poet Yeats said operated like a burning fire of creativity, endowing inspiration, but shortening life. The Scottish name is *leannain-sith*, reputed to be extremely amorous. The Ganconer, or love-talker, is another seductive faery, who can charm the life out of an unwary maiden, similar to *La Belle Dame Sans Merci*. Hugh Mynne, however, takes a different approach, describing how meeting with one's faery lover can bring enlightenment. He does also make the point that such unions are not for everyone and are not to be thoughtlessly sought.

Changelings

There is an old tradition regarding faery thefts of human babies, leaving in their place a changeling and stories in folklore of such happenings are legion. Sadly, the term changeling could be used to ostracize and even abandon offspring who were ugly or deformed in the days when healthy children were an economic necessity. The child could be taken before it was christened. It was common practice to dangle open scissors over the cot, to protect the infant by the cross formation and the presence of iron, which faeries loathe. Sometimes an ancient and withered faery would be left in place of the stolen child, sometimes a stock or simulacrum of the child, that subsequently faded and died. One method of getting an ancient changeling to reveal its age was to make a brew in eggshells, which was supposed to amaze the old faery so much that it would rise up and exclaim that of all the things in heaven and earth it had witnessed, that was the strangest. The changeling might be thrown on to the fire (from where it would rise up the chimney, cackling) or it could be beaten and exposed. Hopefully this would result in the return of the true child, but this did not always happen, and the parents would have to burn thorns on the faery knoll, to induce its return.

Dancing

This is one of the favoured faery activities and all of them seem to enjoy it, from the most exquisite to the most hideous. Stories are told of people who have joined the faeries in their dances and are absent for days or months, while believing they have only been gone an hour. Faeries love music and some tunes are reputed to have been memorized by musicians who listened to the faeries. The *Londonderry Air* is one of them.

ELF SHOT

The faeries were believed to aim flint arrow-heads at certain people and, if they were struck, some illness or disability would follow. Cattle were also targeted.

FAERIES AND FOOD

Faeries love gifts and they like to be offered food, especially milk. It is traditional to leave offerings out for the faeries at Hallowe'en. Faeries take the essence of what is left, not the gross substance. However, do not leave clothes for the faeries, for they will be insulted. If you should find yourself in the land of Faerie, do not touch any food, for if you eat it you will not be able to escape.

FAERY FORTS OR RATHS

These are natural or man-made mounds, usually situated in wild spots. Faeries live within these, passing through and moving within the dense earth, as if it were air. Within the raths they hold court, feast and make merry. They also hold their revels in woodland clearings or beside lonely lakes.

FAERY NAMES

It is traditional to avoid calling the faeries by name, for that may offend and tempt the faeries into malevolence. Because of this they are referred to euphemistically as *The Good People*, *The Fair Folk*, *The Little People*, *The Gentry*, *The Good Neighbours*, *The Forgetful People*, *The Men of Peace*, etc. There are many other names for faeries. The Irish call them the *People of the Sidhe* and other Gaelic variations are *Si* and *Sith*. The deathless, heroic and magical faeries of Ireland are the *Tuatha de Danaan*, the people of the goddess Dana, who in some accounts dwindled to the *Daoine Sidhe*. A Welsh name is *Tylwyth Teg* or *Fair Family*, a Lincolnshire name is *The Strangers*. Bogeys,

hobgoblins, goblins, bogles, phooka and *brag* are some of many varieties of malevolent faery. *Brownies* are helpful little creatures. The *buggane* is a vicious Manx goblin. *Bwbachod* is the Welsh name for brownies. *Knockers* are Cornish mine faeries who are friendly, indicating where the best ore can be found. Their Welsh equivalents are *Coblynau*. In Devon, the *derricks* are believed to lead travellers astray. The *kelpie* is a Scottish bogey appearing in the form of a horse, luring weary travellers on to its back and then rushing into deep water so that they drown. *Pisky* is a mischievous Cornish faery, like other West Country pixies and pigsies, with a puckish sense of humour, having similarities to the Irish leprechaun. A *puck* is a hobgoblin, given individuality in Shakespeare's *A Midsummer Night's Dream*; *pwca* is his Welsh name. *Robin Goodfellow* is a similarly prankish sprite, said by some to be a half-faery. *Seelie Court* and *Unseelie Court* are Scottish terms for faery hosts, kindly and malevolent, respectively. There are many other regional names for a wide variety of faeries, from those who are grotesque and deadly to those who are alluring or helpful. However, all faeries can be dangerous and capricious.

FAERY TERROR

Because of our despoiling of the Earth and her natural resources, and because we disrespect all that is non-physical, even that within our own hearts, mortals and faeries are, in a sense, at war. Many people who regularly stray into deserted places where faeries have their haunts will have experienced faery terror. This is the weapon faeries use to deter the unworthy from approaching their secret spots and it consists of a total blind and unreasoning panic. It is hard not to give in to this, for it is overwhelming, but if you do break into a run, things seem to get worse, and you may get caught in briars and fall over gates until you are well away from the scene. If you feel unwanted it is as well not to trespass in faery territory. If you feel overcome by faery terror, try to be still, visualize yourself surrounded by golden light and send out love, as an offering. You may also employ the protective symbols discussed in *Faeries and Magic*.

Humans and faeries

In general, faeries seem to be wiser and far more powerful than humankind and yet their doings match and mirror human customs and seem intertwined with them. There are instances when faeries have seemed dependent on humans, needing their strength for their sports or battles, needing human artefacts or materials to mend their own tools, needing milk from human mothers, cows and others. Faeries are reported to have their own markets, practise their own arts and crafts, hold their own revels and ride forth in cavalcades. Faeries have been reported to hold their own funerals, although they are more generally believed to be immortal, and such funerals may be a foreshadowing of a human death. Faeries have been known to help and to hinder and to resent intrusions upon their privacy. However, the general impression is that faeries and humans are, in some strange way, interlinked and their fortunes may be entwined.

Joint eater

Also called a just halver, the joint eater attaches itself to a human and feeds on the essence of his or her food, meaning that the unfortunate is always ravenous, always eating and always undernourished. Claire Nahmad (see Further Reading) attributes this to treading on a piece of turf in which an elemental spirit lies in wait. This elemental takes possession of the human, but leaves after a bout of insane gorging. There are ways of tempting forth the invading spirit, given in folklore, such as eating quantities of salt meat and then lying open-mouthed by a running stream, when the joint eater will emerge to take a drink.

Time in faerie

As one might expect with alternative dimensions, time in Faerie passes differently from time in our own world. Sometimes a human may pass many wonderful years in a faery palace, to return whence

he or she came to find only moments have gone by. More often the reverse is true and minutes in the glory of Faerie are months or years by mortal count. People who return from Faerie may find hundreds of years have passed and no one recognizes them. As soon as they make a concrete connection with the world once more, they crumble to dust. However, faery time and human time are mysteriously interlinked and there are times when faeries are more likely to be contacted, such as at the hinges of the day, noon, midnight, dusk and dawn. Certain times of year are also potent and these link with the ancient pagan festivals. Contact is most likely at Samhain, the old Celtic New Year, which coincides now with Hallowe'en. At this time doors between the worlds swing wide. Beltane, or May Eve, is another enchanted time. Midsummer is another powerful faery time, and at the winter solstice, when darkness is at its greatest extent, there may be most danger from malevolent powers. At the autumn equinox also hauntings are very likely.

fURThER REAdING

The Case of the Cottingley Fairies, Joe Cooper, Pocket Books Simon & Schuster Ltd., 1997.
The intriguing story of the Cottingley faeries is here explored, fully and factually.

Fairy Spells, Seeing and Communicating with the Fairies, Claire Nahmad, Souvenir Press, 1997.
A beautifully illustrated and sensitively written account of the faeries, their haunts and preferences, with suggestions for contacting faeries and obtaining healing through them.

A Dictionary of Fairies, Katherine Briggs, Penguin, 1977.
A highly comprehensive, detailed and very readable work on all aspects and types of faery, in tradition and folklore.

A Book of Fairies, Katherine Briggs, Penguin, 1977.
A selection of accounts from faery lore, by this erstwhile president of the English Folklore Society. The contents of this book are drawn from the much longer *Dictionary of Fairies*.

Fairies, Real Encounters with Little People, Janet Bord, Michael O'Mara Books Ltd, 1997.
A fascinating collection of real encounters by this experienced author on the supernatural.

The Faerie Way, Hugh Mynne, Llewellyn, 1998.
This work is highly recommended for those who wish to explore the Faerie tradition and embark on journeys into the world of Faerie and a process of self-transformation. This is a practical and inspiring book of Otherworld experience.

To Hear the Angels Sing, an Odyssey of Co-creation with the Devic Kingdom, Dorothy Maclean, Lindisfarne, 1990.
The full and inspiring story of Findhorn, and how co-operation with nature spirits brought notable results.

The Living World of Faery, R.J. Stewart, Gothic Image, 1995.
Unforgettable accounts, practical instructions and traditional lore, compiled by this contemporary seer and scholar. Highly recommended.

The Fairy Faith in Celtic Countries, W.Y. Evans Wentz, Colin Smythe, 1997.
Compiled in the early years of the twentieth century, this account of experiences with faeries is a classic.

The Celtic Twilight, W.B. Yeats, Prism, 1990.
A collection of mystical tales, accounts and experiences, by the Irish poet and occultist.

The Uses of Enchantment, Bruno Bettelheim, Penguin, 1991.
This work describes how we make use of faery tales to cope with feelings, such as those of anxiety and powerlessness, with special emphasis on how such stories are of psychological help to children. Many traditional tales, such as *Cinderella*, are interpreted.

A BEGINNER'S GUIDE

WITCHCRAFT

Teresa Moorey

f ar from medieval superstition or fairy story,
witchcraft is real, alive and growing. It is a religion
of Nature-worship that exalts the feminine,
encourages individuality and delights in celebration – and
yes, it is also about magic, for magic itself is a natural force.

If you are attracted to the magical and mystical, if you
have ever been alone in the countryside yet felt you were
not alone – or if you are simply curious about natural
forces, this is the book for you.

Witchcraft has much to offer if you practise is sincerely.
It is remarkably ancient, but its message is deeply
meaningful today as we realise how far we have become
estranged from our roots.

spells & rituals

Teresa Moorey

from practical rituals like taking your morning shower to traditions such as lighting candles on your birthday cake, rituals are evident in most aspects of life. Learn to use rituals and spells as a means of focusing your mind, altering your consciousness and bringing about creative change.

Read about:
- seasonal rituals
- rites of passage
- marriage
- blessing
- popular superstitions
- spells

Practice sessions will help to:
- create your own life-changing rituals
- escape from unproductive rituals.

Teresa Moorey is the best-selling author of several books in this beginner's guide series, including *Witchcraft – a beginner's guide*.

A BEGINNER'S GUIDE

PAGANISM

Teresa Moorey

Pagans honour the Goddess, cherish the Earth and respect the traditions and myths of our forbears, seeking to reclaim these where appropriate. Paganism is Nature worship. There are no dogmas, 'shoulds' or 'thou shall nots'; to pagans it is important to celebrate the cycles of life. Most pagans are very ordinary people. They may seek the divine in woodland, by stream or on mountainside, but they also use the modern magic of computers and technology. There are many different forms of paganism, as this book describes, but they are united in their basic attitude and respect for the ways of others.

Have you ever wondered how to recapture a sense of meaning in our synthetic, compartmentalised world, or longed to feel closer to Nature and to your roots? If so, these pages are sure to have something to launch you on your most fascinating quest of all: this is a quest within, to your distant past, to your future possibilities.

A BEGINNER'S GUIDE

hERBS FOR MAGIC AND RITUAL

Teresa Moorey

have you ever felt a fascination for the lore of herbs, or wondered about their properties for natural healing? Perhaps you want to use essential oils, but are unsure where to start. Maybe you would like to make your own incense blends, but feel confused about ingredients.

This book looks at some of the well-known herbs, and the stories attached to them. There is information here to get you started with investigating the allure of essential oils and their many qualities for healing and pleasure. Clear, practical information is given on inexpensive incense blends. More than this you can discover simple ways to activate your own healing and magical abilities.

Herbs for Magic and Ritual is intended to start you off on your own exploration of the meanings of herbs, in their simplicity and beauty. You may discover that this is life-enhancing, satisfying and compelling. As gifts of Nature there is little to compare with herbs – they are there for us to enjoy.